**WITHDRAWN**

# THE ELEMENTARY SCHOOL LIBRARY

Margaret L. Brewer
and
Sharon O. Willis

The Shoe String Press, Inc.
1970

Copyright © 1970 by Margaret L. Brewer and Sharon O. Willis

ISBN: 0-208-01092-0
Library of Congress Catalog Card Number: 77-127793

Printed in the United States of America

# CONTENTS

      LIST OF ILLUSTRATIONS . . . . . . . . . . . . . . . . . . . . . . . . .iv

      PREFACE . . . . . . . . . . . . . . . . . . . . . . . . . . . . . . . . . . . . . .v

  I. HISTORY OF THE ELEMENTARY SCHOOL LIBRARY  1

 II. PHILOSOPHY OF THE ELEMENTARY SCHOOL LIBRARY . . . . . . . . . . . . . . . . . . . . . . . . . . . . . . . . . . . .9

III. FUNCTIONS OF THE ELEMENTARY SCHOOL . . . . . . .12

IV. STAFFING THE ELEMENTARY SCHOOL LIBRARY . . .21

 V. ADMINISTRATIVE ORGANIZATION OF ELEMENTARY SCHOOL LIBRARIES . . . . . . . . . . . . . .25

VI. ADMINISTRATION OF TECHNICAL PROCESSES . . . .29

VII. ORGANIZATION OF PUBLIC SERVICES IN THE ELEMENTARY SCHOOL LIBRARY . . . . . . . . . . . . . . . .46

VIII. PHYSICAL FACILITIES . . . . . . . . . . . . . . . . . . . . . . . . .52

IX. ORGANIZATION AND ADMINISTRATION OF MULTIMEDIA RESOURCES . . . . . . . . . . . . . . . . . . . . .61

 X. EVALUATION OF THE ELEMENTARY SCHOOL LIBRARY . . . . . . . . . . . . . . . . . . . . . . . . . . . . .73

      APPENDIXES . . . . . . . . . . . . . . . . . . . . . . . . . . . . . . . . . .77

      SELECTED BIBLIOGRAPHY . . . . . . . . . . . . . . . . . . . . .101

      INDEX . . . . . . . . . . . . . . . . . . . . . . . . . . . . . . . . . . . . . .107

## LIST OF ILLUSTRATIONS

1. Library Instruction Schedule . . . . . . . . . . . . . . . . . . . . . . . . . . . . 17
2. Library Request Form . . . . . . . . . . . . . . . . . . . . . . . . . . . . . . . . 30
3. Multiple Order Form . . . . . . . . . . . . . . . . . . . . . . . . . . . . . . . . 34
4. Cataloging Workslip . . . . . . . . . . . . . . . . . . . . . . . . . . . . . . . . . 36
5. Main Entry Diagram . . . . . . . . . . . . . . . . . . . . . . . . . . . . . . . . 39
6. Set of Typed Catalog Cards . . . . . . . . . . . . . . . . . . . . . . . . . . . . 40-41
7. Typed Pocket, Book Card, Date Due Slip . . . . . . . . . . . . . . . . 42
8. Elementary School Library Floor Plan . . . . . . . . . . . . . . . . . . 53-54
9. Chart of Furnishings . . . . . . . . . . . . . . . . . . . . . . . . . . . . . . . . 55-56
10. Periodical Holdings Card . . . . . . . . . . . . . . . . . . . . . . . . . . . . 64
11. Multimedia Main Entry Cards . . . . . . . . . . . . . . . . . . . . . . . . 66-68
12. Temporary Charge Slip . . . . . . . . . . . . . . . . . . . . . . . . . . . . . 72

# PREFACE

*The Elementary School Library* is intended for use by the librarian, the school administrator, as well as the volunteer parent. Its object is to provide a theoretical and practical introduction to the administration and organization of the elementary school library. The modern school curriculum demands an abundance of print and non-print material to enrich its library program, and it is the authors opinion that no gaps should exist between kindergarten and the high school in the organization of a school library program. This book is an attempt to assist librarians, school librarians, and interested parents in the initial and perhaps the most important part of this task.

The authors are indebted to the following persons: John Gordon Burke, for his guidance, editorial assistance and criticism in the preparation of this manuscript; Carolee Porter McKinstry, for clerical assistance; our husbands, for their assistance with illustrations and content analysis. Acknowledgement is also made to Demco for allowing use of their materials.

# I

# HISTORY OF THE ELEMENTARY SCHOOL LIBRARY

Americans cannot claim to be the first to establish and recommend the use of book collections in the primary grades. The idea of placing a library in the elementary school can be traced back to Europe. According to "Rapports des agents du ministre de l'interieur dan des departments," a small collection of books was to be placed in each school for the use of the pupils.[1] This collection was to be under the care of the school administrator known as "Instituteur." By the latter 1800's there were more than a million volumes in the school libraries of France.

The idea of providing space, books and teachers in schools in America can be traced as far as the 1630's to the West India Company in the Dutch colony of New Netherland.[2] When the English seized New York in 1664, they did little to further the continuance of public education and libraries. However, book collections in existence continued as collections in the private Dutch schools.

The French development of elementary school libraries influenced the United States during the early 1800's when Governor DeWitt Clinton of New York visited Europe. It was Clinton's stay in France which caused him, no doubt, to place the school library in a position of prominence in his educational ideals. Governor Clinton recommended the formation of better school systems to the New

---

[1] France. Ministère de l'intérieur, *Rapports des agents du ministre de l'intérieur dan des départments* (1793-anII) Collection de documents inédits sur l'historie de France pub par les soins du ministre de l'instruction on publique. Paris: Impr. National, 1913-51. (2v)

[2] Michigan University, Clements Library, *Education in Early America*, (Bulletin 73). Ann Arbor: University of Michigan, 1967, p.6.

York legislature in 1827. One of his proposals for better schools was that a "small library of books should be placed in every school house."[3] Though Clinton was outspoken in support of school libraries, it was not until 1835 that the voters of New York passed a law permitting school districts to levy a tax specifically for library use. The school district libraries, as they were called, grew rapidly. However, authority was granted in 1843 that permitted the library fund to be used for the purchase of school equipment and payments of teachers' wages. At that time, 125 books were the minimum recommended for the districts containing 50 children or less. After 1860, the number of volumes held by schools steadily declined so that by 1874 the superintendent's report indicated only 831,554 volumes.[4] In the same report the superintendent recommended the repeal of the law of 1835. Thus began a gradual decline of elementary school libraries in New York.

The development of libraries in New York was characteristic of school library development in other Northern and New England states. During the period 1835-1860, nineteen states passed legislation to promote public school libraries. With the advent of the Civil War, schools and their libraries were deprived of funds as well as personnel and facilities. Library development was slow in commencing again. However, other forces were making the elementary school library an essential part of the total school program. Primarily, the educational philosophy was changing from a "textbook" approach of teaching to an exploratory unit approach. The success of the latter methods depended upon an abundance and variety of supplementary materials in the school and these were most logically placed in a central library.

By 1890, however, few elementary school libraries existed. Evidence to support this fact appeared when the United States Office of Education made its first report on libraries in the United States.[5]

---

[3] Henry L. Cecil, *School Library Service in the United States,* New York: H. W. Wilson, 1940, P. 42.

[4] New York. Superintendent of Public Instruction, *Twenty-First Annual Report.* New York: Department of Public Instruction, 1875, p. 26-27.

[5] U.S. Bureau of Education, "Public, Society, and School Libraries," *Report of the Commissioner of Education for the year 1899-1900,* Chapter XVII. Washington: Government Printing Office, 1901.

## THE ELEMENTARY SCHOOL LIBRARY IN THE 20th CENTURY

Room libraries were the prevalent type of book collections in 1900. While some schools had been cooperating with public libraries to bring library service to their pupils, others had purchased books from their school funds and placed them in individual classrooms. The latter plan was a common development in the elementary school; the teachers favored the room library because they felt they could more or less supervise what the children read. The National Education Association recommended that "A collection of fifty books in a room chosen with reference to the age and ability of the pupils in that room is the most satisfactory means of forming a taste for good literature."[6]

The great turning point for elementary school library development in this century came with the publication of the *Fourth Yearbook of the NEA, Department of Elementary School Principals* "Elementary School Library Standards," 1925, and later published by the American Library Association. It is clear that this publication paved the way for development of centralized elementary school libraries. Known generally as the companion to the "Certain Report," elementary school library standards were spelled out in full. Mr. Certain emphasized that,

> Certainly no other factor in school organization bears more directly upon educational environment than does the library. When one considers how seriously a school may be cluttered up by the introduction of magazines and newspapers into classrooms, or how seriously work may be interrupted through haphazard introduction into a classroom of moving pictures, stereopticons, or victrola records, he will appreciate the importance of having a centralized agency for storing these materials where they may be readily available exactly at the time when they are needed.[7]

The standards were very comprehensive, covering a definition of the library, a book collection, architectural specifications,

---

[6] Clarissa Newcomb, "Schoolroom Libraries," *National Education Association of the U.S., Addresses and Proceedings.* Washington: NEA, 1899, p. 527.

[7] C. C. Certain, "Report of the Joint Committee on Elementary School Library Standards," *Fourth Yearbook of the NEA Department of Elementary School Principals.* Washington: NEA, 1925, p. 327.

administrative requirements, library instruction, budget, and a basic list of 212 books for the beginning elementary school library. It was Mr. Certain's opinion that no school was too poor to afford a centralized elementary library. Through his encouragement and practical illustrations of how a library can be organized with a few dollars, the development of elementary school libraries progressed. One must not conclude as a result of the "Certain Report," every school in the nation set high priorities on school library services. This did not happen for several reasons; two of the most important being that during the depression of the 1930's appropriations for reading materials were left entirely out of the school budget or they were a relatively small item, and school administrators hesitated in initiating a school library program for each elementary school.

Following the "Certain Report," various special committees of professional organizations began to make school libraries the subject of careful study. One of the more important of these studies was undertaken by the Southern Association of Colleges and Secondary Schools. Several studies were made during the 1930's on the state level; some of the better state studies published were those of Illinois, Massachusetts, New York, and Iowa. These studies were sponsored, in most instances, by the State Departments of Education in cooperation with state library associations.

By 1940, ten states had developed some guidelines for the development of elementary school libraries.[8] The publication and availability of guidelines for use by school systems undoubtedly influenced the building of elementary school library collections of books; but these publications did not contain provisions for the qualifications for library personnel nor for the physical facilities of the library. Statistics for 1940 indicate that there were 954 full-time elementary school librarians employed in the public schools of the United States, but a total of 5,165 centralized elementary libraries were reported to be in existence. In 1940 slightly over eight percent of the schools in the 94,254 elementary school systems in the United States had no type of library service.[9]

[8] U.S. Office of Education, "School Library Standards, 1954," *U. S. Office of Education Bulletin, 1954, No. 15.* Washington: Government Printing Office, 1954, p.11.

[9] U. S. Office of Education, "Statistics of Public School Libraries," *Biennial Survey of Education in the U.S., 1941-42.* Washington: Government Printing Office, Vol. VIII, 1945, pp. 21, 14, 11; Vol. IV, 1944, p. 50.

In 1945, with the publication of *School Libraries for Today and Tomorrow,* the American Library Association published a national set of minimum recommendations for school library development.[10] Although these guidelines were not detailed, they did present an organized approach toward school library development. These standards were general guidelines for the development of all types of school libraries.

Definite progress in library development was made after the publication of *School Libraries for Today and Tomorrow.* However, in 1954 the U. S. Office of Education issued a statistical publication which alarmed the American Library Association, the American Association of School Librarians, the National Education Association, and the National Council of Teachers of English. At that time, forty-six states had developed some guidelines for the improvement of libraries on the secondary school level. However, only 30 had made any definite recommendations for the elementary school library.[11] Approximately 75 percent of the elementary schools were without school library services. Although classroom collections and other types of library service provided limited resources, they were in no way equivalent to centralized elementary school libraries. Millions of children were without elementary school library services.

## FINANCIAL STIMULATION FOR SCHOOL LIBRARIES

The first financial incentive for elementary school library development came from the Carnegie Corporation in the early 1930's and was later supplemented by funds from the Julius Rosenwald Fund. Although much of the Carnegie support went for public libraries, the Rosenwald grants were directed toward development of Negro elementary and high school libraries in the South.

With the passage of the National Defense Education Act in 1958, funds were made available to schools for the primary purpose of building resource materials for various curriculum areas. Elemen-

---

[10] American Library Association, *School Libraries for Today and Tomorrow.* Chicago: American Library Association, 1945.

[11] U. S. Office of Education, "School Library Standards, 1954," *U. S. Office of Education Bulletin, 1954, No. 15.* Washington: Government Printing Office, 1954, pp. 4, 11.

tary schools, as well as high schools, were eligible to apply for these funds. Thousands of elementary school systems in the United States received money as a result of the National Defense Education Act. Books and laboratory materials purchased with these funds had to be housed, supervised, and catalogued in accordance with the National Defense Education Act rules, and the administrator was held responsible for knowing where all materials purchased with these funds were located. Most elementary schools did not have libraries. This meant make-shift adjustments had to be made within many schools to accomodate the materials. The *Standards for School Library Programs,* published in 1960, states the basic requirements for truly functional school library programs in the form of both qualitative and quantitative standards.[12] These standards have been used as guides in most states in appraising existing library situations and in formulating long-range plans for library development. Although these standards mention the elementary school library in particular, they do not contain a comprehensive coverage of the elementary library. Even so, school systems, individual schools, and State Departments of Education have gained immeasurable guidance from the 1960 standards. Many states have formulated their own standards based on regional standards and the American Library Association's standards.

The new *Standards for School Media Programs,* published in 1969, provides school systems with quantitative recommendations for the major resources and facilities and equipment for school libraries serving all grade levels, K-12.[13] In general, the same recommendations apply to elementary, junior high, and high schools. These recommendations integrate the entire instructional resources of the school into a centrally administered school media program. Although resources, facilities and equipment recommendations are well identified, other aspects of the total administrative and organizational structure of the media program are less detailed and hence are less recognizable as recommendations. These "standards," used in conjunction with the "1960 standards," provide rather high goals for which schools should strive. As yet, the new stand-

[12] American Association of School Librarians, *Standards for School Library Programs.* Chicago: American Library Association, 1960.

[13] American Library Association, *Standards for School Media Programs.* Chicago: American Library Association, 1969.

ards are too recent to have a measurable impact on the development of libraries.

In 1966 there were 73,216 elementary school systems,[14] with 31.4 percent having central library facilities. Statistics indicate that 19,000 school districts in the United States and its possessions have received federal funds since 1965.[15] Not only have there been new materials placed in school libraries, but the number of qualified librarians on the elementary level has also increased. There is, however, a severe shortage of personnel. This will undoubtedly continue to be true as historically the demand for qualified personnel seems to always outweigh supply. To meet these shortages, many colleges are offering specialized course work to prepare elementary school librarians. Several of the colleges accredited by the American Library Association provide graduate work in which one may specialize in the area of elementary school librarianship; along with this program there are similar offerings for preparation as instructional materials specialists.

Tremendous growth in elementary school library development began in 1965 with the Elementary and Secondary Education Act. This act was keyed to poverty, and virtually doubled the amount of federal aid available to public schools. There were five provisions in the bill. Title I provided funds for local school districts through state education agencies, which educated children from low income families. Title II authorized distribution of funds to the states for acquisition of library resources, including textbooks and audio-visual materials. Title III provided grants to local school districts for the establishment of supplementary education centers. Title IV made funds available for development of regional educational research and training facilities. Title V provided funds to strengthen State Departments of Education.[16]

The Elementary and Secondary Education Act of 1965 has produced a faster growth of elementary school libraries than any previous stimulus. This growth resulted in greater quantity and quality

[14] U. S. Office of Education, *Digest of Educational Statistics, 1968*. Washington: Government Printing Office, 1968, p. 46.

[15] U. S. Office of Education, *Profile of the Elementary and Secondary Education Act of 1965*. Washington: Government Printing Office, 1967, p. 7.

[16] Buckman Osborne, "Schoolman's Guide to Federal Aid," *School Management,* IX:65, 1965.

of library materials and the development of school library standards in many of the fifty states. It also resulted in the establishment of some centralized elementary school libraries and funded the appointment of state school library supervisors in many states. Upon the expiration of the Elementary and Secondary Education Act, solid foundations will have been made by State Departments of Education, as well as local school districts, for the establishment of elementary school libraries in every school district in the country.

# II

# PHILOSOPHY OF THE ELEMENTARY SCHOOL LIBRARY

Every school library needs a philosophy. The library's philosophy should contain three parts: the general philosophical statement explaining the theoretical basis for the library; the long-range purposes which identify the major phases of service that will be rendered in fulfillment of the philosophy; and broad objectives which designate types of service and identify the role of the librarian.

Many school districts have school library supervisors who are responsible for library development in all the schools in the district. In such cases, the formation of the philosophy of the school library is the responsibility of this person. However, when a school library district supervisor does not exist, the elementary school librarian should assume the responsibility of forming a committee for the purpose of preparing a library philosophy. The librarian should act as chairman of the committee and the school administrator should assist him in recommending other teachers and a member of the administrative staff to be on the committee. Normally, a five-person committee is advisable; larger committees can easily stray from the work at hand. Several meetings of the committee will be necessary and should be arranged on a regular schedule.

Individual committee members should be expected to conduct research and investigation. The following steps should initially be taken by the committee: A study made of all national statements dealing with school library philosophies; a study made of state publications dealing with school libraries and their administration; a study made of all local school district handbooks on school libraries and all local statements on school library philosophy; and a review of the curriculum guides issued for the elementary school on both the state and local level. Having taken these steps, the committee is ready to proceed with the composition of the philosophical statement for the school library. An example of an elementary school library philosophy is contained in Appendix I.

The purposes of the elementary school library should evolve from the school library philosophy. The purposes of the library, like those of the school system, should be formulated according to current educational philosophies. The Educational Policies Commission,[1] commends that the principles of self-realization, creative human relationships, economic efficiency, and civic responsibility should be applied to the major functions of the elementary school library. In determining the purposes of a school library, the committee should be aware of school district library development, and know the strata of the community the school serves. Appendix I provides an example of the relationship of a school library's purposes to its philosophy.

After formulation of the purposes of the elementary school library, the committee should delineate a set of objectives. The objectives as developed by the American Library Association in 1945 still serve as an excellent model in planning and implementing a school library program. As devised by the American Library Association, the objectives of the school library are to

> Participate effectively in the school program as it strives to meet the needs of pupils, teachers, parents, and other community members.
> Provide boys and girls with the library materials and services most appropriate and most meaningful in their growth and development as individuals.
> Stimulate and guide pupils in all phases of their reading so that they may find increasing enjoyment and satisfaction and may grow in critical judgment and appreciation.
> Provide an opportunity through library experiences for boys and girls to develop helpful interests, to make satisfactory personal adjustments, and to acquire desirable social attitudes.
> Help children and young people become skillful and discriminating users of libraries and of printed and audio-visual materials.
> Introduce pupils to community libraries as early as possible and cooperate with those libraries in their efforts to encourage

---

[1] Educational Policies Commission, *The Purposes of Education in American Democracy*. Washington: National Education Association, 1938, p. 47.

## PHILOSOPHY OF THE ELEMENTARY SCHOOL LIBRARY

continuing education and cultural growth.

Work with teachers in the selection and use of all types of library materials which contribute to the teaching program.

Cooperate with other librarians and community leaders in planning and developing an overall library program for the community or area.[2]

The objectives of the school library should be based on the functional areas of the elementary school library; administration, organization of library materials, library use, and reading guidance. The committee should develop its own objectives, making them especially applicable to the school, but using the objectives developed by the American Library Association as a model. An example of an individual school's objectives may also be found in Appendix I.

Having completed the philosophical statement, the purposes and objectives of the elementary school library, the work of the committee as a whole is ended until a revision is needed in updating the library with the school's program. Now is the time for the librarian to assume full responsibility in carrying out the objectives set forth by the committee endorsed by the school administrator.

In order for the librarian to perform functions that fulfill the objectives of the school library, he should develop short term aims. An aim is a task that the librarian can accomplish within a given period of time. Some examples of aims are to arrange for cooperative projects by the public and school library, to make use of special reading displays in the library and in the school, to emphasize National Library Week and National Education Week with an open house and special book talks, and to sponsor special speakers. Aims should be planned so that they can be realized on a semester basis. The librarian will be wise to try to accomplish programmed aims before adding new ones. Endowed with a well-planned philosophy, purposes, objectives and aims, the librarian is ready to administer a well-organized library in the school program.

---

[2] American Library Association, Committee on Post-War Planning, *School Libraries for Today and Tomorrow.* Chicago: ALA, 1945, pp. 9-10.

# III

# FUNCTIONS OF THE ELEMENTARY SCHOOL LIBRARY

The functions of the elementary school library may be divided into four service areas: (1) reading for pleasure, (2) reading guidance, (3) instruction in the use of the library, and (4) instruction in implementation of research methods.

## READING FOR PLEASURE

Reading for pleasure, or free reading, refers to the reading done by students other than special assignments made by the teacher. Free reading, or reading by self-selection, should form a large percentage of what each child reads daily. Free reading is a many-faceted thing. Every person with whom the child comes in contact will, to some degree, influence his reading. The home, the community, and the school remain the primary sources of influence.

When the child enters school, his first acquaintance with an adult is normally his home room teacher. His second adult acquaintance should be the librarian. The librarian should arrange for a cooperative program of library services to the classroom. Normally, a collection of books will be provided in the classroom that enriches and supplements the current unit of study. The librarian should encourage the teacher to make arrangements in his lesson plans so that the librarian can come to the classroom for participation in story telling or a "show and tell" session. Following this session, the librarian should invite the students and teacher to come to the library. In an informal first visit, the students learn the location of the library, meet the librarian, and already are aware of some of the things the librarian can do for them. This is the right beginning for the student's acceptance and appreciation of the library and its services.

Once the librarian and teacher have developed a desire to read by the student, the librarian's major responsibility rests in the guidance of reading selections. All students want to learn; the degrees to which they are capable and the rate at which they learn are the only governing agents in this matter. It is very essential that the desire to learn is never dulled. The teacher and librarian should seize every opportunity to enrich the reading experience of their students. At times, the librarian and teacher may want to enter special pleas with parents to assist and reinforce the patterns of reading recommended at school.

## READING GUIDANCE

Reading guidance is a cooperative endeavor by both the teacher and librarian. The librarian should know the book collection, the magazines, and the multi-media in the library. It is his obligation to become acquainted with the individual interests of the children through use of school records and visitations with teachers and students. The basic principles which the librarian should observe in providing reading guidance are a thorough knowledge of the book collection, a personal knowledge of the children, and the provision of opportunities for the children to use the facilities of the library.

The librarian should have a thorough knowledge of the book collection with which he works. He should read constantly in the book collection of the library. The more books he knows personally, the more effective reading guidance becomes and the more confidence the children will have in his suggestions. One of the essentials of interesting children in books comes as an outgrowth of the librarian's own personal enthusiasm for books and reading.

Knowing the students requires a genuine interest in young people and a sympathetic understanding of their problems. It also involves studying the student's interests, aptitudes, and hobbies. It may require consultation with teachers or principals. The librarian should know the reading ability of every student accurately enough to assist him in selecting materials which he can read. The librarian's task is to try to analyze skillfully the background, the intersts, and the needs of each individual and to try to supply him with suitable library materials. The slow-reading child or the reluctant reader requires careful attention and real patience. The librarian must gain his complete confidence. Books which are simply written, mature in content, with large type, and containing profuse illustrations are appealing to the slow reader. The gifted child also needs the librarian's help. The library may offer the only outlet for the gifted child's interests and abilities. Most gifted children will pursue a wide variety of reading without any special encouragement. The librarian may be the first person to notice that preoccupation with books is depriving a gifted child of normal social development; therefore, the librarian is in a good position to help him broaden his interests into active participation in suitable group activities.

Browsing plays an important part in the student's reading. Students need some guidance in browsing, however, so that it does not become a major time-consuming activity. The librarian can help students browse intelligently by regularly offering a few simple suggestions: look at the author's name to see if he is a familiar author; look at the name of the illustrator to see if he is well known; look at the pictures to see if they are interesting, or read the description of the book which may be pasted on the inside of the cover.

Reading guidance involves the application of bibliotherapy, especially for the emotionally disturbed child. The problem can range from rowdiness to shyness and withdrawal. Specific guidance from the librarian can become a positive factor in helping students with personality adjustments and it can also help in the development of wholesome ideals and basic principles of conduct. The assumption is by reading the proper books, the student will identify himself with a character who faces a problem or a situation similar to his own. Through this identification, attitudes and behavior can be influenced so that the student may adjust to his own situation satisfactorily.

Techniques for rendering reading guidance fall into two categories: individual guidance and group guidance.

GROUP GUIDANCE. Group guidance is, by far the easier type of guidance for the librarian and through it the greatest number of students can be reached. Book talks can be given about new books, books in a single category (such as hobbies), books related to current class work, and about books that appeal to a particular group of students.

Well planned exhibits fall into group guidance and can be centered around units of study, seasonal themes, or other topics that arouse curiosity for reading. Books, as well as book jackets and other

# FUNCTIONS OF THE ELEMENTARY SCHOOL LIBRARY

visual materials, may be used for the exhibits. Often class work is an excellent way to form an exhibit and create interest for related reading materials.

Specific story hours should be scheduled for all children from nursery school through sixth grade. These story hours can serve a definite purpose in group guidance. The younger children should be started on stories approximately five minutes in length, while the older children's story hour can extend to 30 minutes. The story hour can combine reading stories with story telling or showing picture books, and discussion of illustrations. Children enjoy sharing stories and recommending good books for others to enjoy. Many times the recommendation coming from another child is much more acceptable to the children than an adult's recommendation. In such sessions, the librarian will be careful to phrase questions carefully in directing the exchange of ideas and not let the session stray from the original subject content.

Additional group guidance can take the form of audio-visual materials, such as tape recordings, films, and illustrations used in presenting stories or in connection with books, book games (from the guessing games to elaborate quizzes which are play activities) that encourage children to become acquainted with stories and poems, and dramatizations which provide activities for entire class participation. This may range from simply acting out the story to more advanced drama, charades, or marionette shows. Dioramas and puppet shows are also very effective.

INDIVIDUAL GUIDANCE. The majority of the students will benefit from group guidance, but there will still be many who need special help from the librarian, the teacher and the guidance counselor. Those students who have not responded to group guidance should be spotted by the teacher and librarian. Individual guidance should be primarily directed toward those students who are identified as slow learners or the gifted. The average reader also may have need for individual guidance at times.

The slow reader normally has little interest in reading; this may be caused by below normal intelligence, or it could be caused by poor vision or some other physical handicap. Regardless of the cause, the librarian and teacher are concerned with encouraging the child to read so that he can maximize his abilities. Some techniques that can be used are reading aloud, art and craft activities following a story, and story telling by the students.

The accelerated learner may display some of the same symptoms as the slow learner, but his disinterest will stem from lack of appropriate reading materials and related media. Special programs planned through the library can have far-reaching effects on the exceptionally bright child. Some examples of activities are the use of the tape recorder for students to tape and play back stories of their own, book reports stressing the fundamentals of structure and presentation, and formation of a Literary Club in which the students hold regular meetings, learn parliamentary procedure, and plan programs of their own choosing.

The average reader has need for guidance in his reading habits too. One of the most noticeable habits of the average reader is an inability to vary his reading. Through the use of reading records, the librarian and the teacher can determine the actual reading habits of the student. Steering the student to other types of reading is a task not easily accomplished. Reading suggestions must be tactfully made and the librarian must let the student know that he is personally interested in the books the student reads. When a student borrows a book which the librarian or a friend has suggested, the librarian should endeavor to get the child's reaction to the book when he returns it. From this discussion, new interests can be developed.

## INSTRUCTION IN THE USE OF THE LIBRARY

Instruction in how to use the library is a cooperative endeavor which involves the support of the school administrator and coordination of activity by the teacher and the librarian. A regular course of study in library science should be developed and carried out under the direction of the librarian. It should contain the following: philosophy of the library, objectives, units of work by grade level, and suggested methods and techniques by which the units are to be implemented. The course of study should cover all grades served by the library. For each grade, units of work should be organized so that a continuous and coordinated instructional program in the library will exist from grades K-9. Appendix II provides a developmental sequence of library skills for grades K-9. Based on library skills by grade level, an example of a unit to be presented in the kindergarten is outlined in Appendix III.

Library instruction may be formal or informal, but the best program of instruction will be a planned combination of the two.

# FUNCTIONS OF THE ELEMENTARY SCHOOL LIBRARY 17

| Student:<br>Grade:<br>Hour: | John<br>2<br>8:30 | Alice<br>6<br>9:00 | Tom<br>7<br>9:30 | 10:00 | 10:30 | 11:00 | 12:30 | 1:00 | 1:30 | 2:00 | 2:30 | 3:00 |
|---|---|---|---|---|---|---|---|---|---|---|---|---|
| How to use card catalog | | | | | | | | | | | | |
| How to use encyclopedia | | | | | | | | | | | | |
| How to use dictionary | | | | | | | | | | | | |
| Find book on shelf | | | | | | | | | | | | |
| Check books in | | | | | | | | | | | | |
| Check books out | | | | | | | | | | | | |
| File circulation cards | | | | | | | | | | | | |
| Shelve books | | | | | | | | | | | | |
| Read shelves | | | | | | | | | | | | |
| Tell stories | | | | | | | | | | | | |
| Read stories & poetry | | | | | | | | | | | | |
| Prepare overdue notices | | | | | | | | | | | | |
| Plan displays | | | | | | | | | | | | |
| Shelve magazines | | | | | | | | | | | | |
| Help others use library | | | | | | | | | | | | |
| Use of Reader's Guide | | | | | | | | | | | | |
| Use of indexes | | | | | | | | | | | | |
| Taking notes | | | | | | | | | | | | |

HOW TO USE CHECKLIST:

To use this checklist effectively, each student, grades 2-6, should come into the library for individual instruction a minimum of 5 hrs. a year. A proven method is for the teachers and librarian to decide when a certain student, (eventually all students during the year) can come in the library for instruction at a certain time each day, ½ hr. per day for 2 weeks. This provides an "on the job learning program" for the student. As a student performs a task or completes a learning experience, the librarian can check the appropriate square. At all times, the librarian and teacher have a record.

*Illustration No. 1. Library Instruction Schedule.*

Formal instruction in use of the library normally takes two forms: group instruction and individual instruction.

GROUP INSTRUCTION. Group instruction on a formal basis is most often used. In order for group instruction to be effective, the librarian must use a prepared course of study in the use of the library. He must also arrange a schedule to fit other library use activities. Group instruction should have direct follow-ups on use of the library. In this connection, teachers can utilize regular library visitation periods, and place extra emphasis on library skills in the classroom.

INDIVIDUAL INSTRUCTION. The ideal situation for instruction in use of the library provides individual instruction for each student. This type of instruction allows for individual differences, varying interests, various rates of learning, and necessary reinforcement. Many schools are utilizing individual instruction in their regular classrooms. In such situations, the librarian should be able to perform the individualized library instruction easily through cooperation with each teacher. To formalize individual instruction in use of the library in schools where a program of individual instruction is not present, the following program is recommended.

The librarian should arrange a schedule with all teachers so each student comes to the library for an instruction period. During the course of a school year, each student can receive individual instruction in library skills. To implement this program, a schedule such as the one illustrated in Illustration No. 1 should be devised. The student should come to the library for instruction for one-half hour each day for a week. The librarian should let him assist in doing any of the tasks listed in Illustration No. 1 that he is capable of doing. All students above grade 2 should be allowed in the program. At the end of the first week, another group of students should start the instructional period. A determination must be made as to how many students can effectively be managed at one time in this type of learning situation. If the librarian works alone and has no assistance, no more than three students at one time are recommended. If clerical help is available, then a proportionate number of additional students should be allowed. By the end of the year, depending on the number of library personnel, about 500 to 1,500 students can receive instruction in this manner.

INFORMAL INSTRUCTION. Informal instruction in use of the library is quite often the only type of instruction in library skills

# FUNCTIONS OF THE ELEMENTARY SCHOOL LIBRARY

received by the student. The informal instruction may take place in the school, in the library, or even through the public library. If the librarian favors the informal type of instruction, then he is obligated to provide each teacher with a list of the skills by grade level on use of the library. Further, it would be wise to give the public librarian in your town or city a copy. If the librarian is the only employee in the school library, he will not have time to provide an individualized instructional program to the school. If this is the case, the librarian should utilize the group type of formal instruction if such a group program can be worked out satisfactorily.

COOPERATIVE INSTRUCTIONAL PROGRAMS. A school library can carry out its instructional program best when there is genuine cooperation between the classroom teacher, the librarian, and the public librarian. A formal program carried out by either the librarian or the teacher, supplemented by the efforts of other teachers and the public librarian, yields excellent benefits.

## INDEPENDENT RESEARCH

A function of the elementary school library is also that of guiding children in research study. The philosophy behind this function is aptly summarized in *Using Reference Materials Effectively in Schools.*

> This independent study approach should not be seen as a revival of the project method or as another form of supervised study. It refers to a plan of teaching which deliberately aims at instructing an individual learner in his independent study activities. Such study may or may not be an extension of units of work under way in the total class. Nor is this just a plan for able students. The poor and reluctant learners are those most in need of the teacher's patience and skill to get them started on their own. Whatever the arrangement, the essential ingredients are: A question, a problem, or some other task important to the learner; the guidance, as needed, of the teacher or other resource person to provide 'human feedback;' and the necessary materials, time and other facilities to carry on the learning task involved . . . Whatever approach is used, the learner needs a variety of excellent materials readily available to him.[1]

---

[1] Field Enterprises Educational Corp., *Using Reference Materials Effectively in Schools.* Lincoln, Nebr.: University of Nebraska, 1967, p. 3.

Some educators and librarians call research "use of reference books," but this infers an undesirable meaning. Reference books normally mean those encyclopedias and handbooks which the librarian has classed "reference." Research really means exploration of available resources to form an opinion on a topic or a specific item. Research to one student may be the use of a dictionary for a short interpretation of a word. To another student, research will be the use of all the available books, periodicals, encyclopedias, newspapers and various multi-media materials to formulate an opinion about an item or topic. In the cultivation of individual research, the librarian should discourage students from always seeking an answer in a single book. Even the first grader should be encouraged to use several books. The child inquiring about the habits of the woodhen would find books, films, filmstrips, tape recordings, posters and realia of equal importance in formulating his concepts.

At every instance, the classroom teacher should encourage the children to do research and answer the many questions they raise in class. The teacher is the important key in individual research. Any time during the school day when questions arise to which his students desire answers, a teacher should encourage them to seek information. The ideal situation is to have the most commonly used reference sources available in the classrooms. For more extensive research, the student should be urged to go to the library. Upon arrival at the library, the librarian should be on hand to provide individual guidance to the student in his search for information. When the child returns to the classroom with the information, he should be allowed to share with the class his findings. Further, he should be encouraged to tell the class how they can find this information. Through encouragement, reward, and motivation, the child at an early age can become self-confident in research methods and in the use of the library.

# IV

# STAFFING THE ELEMENTARY SCHOOL LIBRARY

School systems should base their needs for professional librarians on the American Library Association's *Standards for School Media Programs*. According to the American Library Association, one media specialist is recommended for each 250 students.[1] Schools should also consult guidelines available in the state or their local district. For further qualifications of the librarian the regional accrediting association's "guidelines" relative to the elementary school library can be reviewed.

The recommendations concerning the professional education of school librarians in the American Library Association's standards are qualitative. The school librarian should have a broad, general education and should meet the certification requirements of his state, regional accrediting association and of the school system. An elementary school librarian ideally should be especially trained for children's library work.

Every elementary school librarian must first of all be a teacher and maintain those traits and characteristics expected of an elementary school teacher. Primary traits which should characterize a teacher are enthusiasm, cheerfulness, an understanding of pupils, and flexibility.[2] Additional personal traits expected of a librarian are adeptness in human relations, a thorough understanding of the curriculum,

---

[1] American Library Association, *Op. Cit.*, p. 12. (According to the new standards, a media specialist can be a librarian, an audiovisual person, a curriculum materials specialist, etc.)

[2] A list of twenty additional characteristics is provided in David G. Ryans, *Characteristics of Teachers*. Washington: American Council on Education, 1960, p. 82.

an extensive knowledge of books and other instructional materials, an enthusiasm for books and reading, a broad background knowledge of all phases of librarianship, and administrative ability.[3]

It is the responsibility of the librarian to administer, organize, and supervise the elementary school library, and its materials and services. In fulfilling this responsibility, the librarian should select and maintain an appropriate collection of books and other library materials for the use of students, maintain a collection of professional books, periodicals and curriculum materials for the use of teachers and administrative staff, participate in curriculum development by serving on the curriculum committee, and provide guidance to pupils by encouraging their use of the library.

## CLERICAL AND/OR SECRETARIAL ASSISTANTS

The clerical assistant, along with secretarial help, is needed in the school library so that the librarian can spend most of his time working with teachers and students. The number of clerical assistants recommended by the American Library Association is as follows: One aide and one technician for each media specialist in schools of 2,000 students or fewer.[4] The number of clerical assistants may also be determined by standards for one's regional accrediting association and state department of education.

The duties of the library clerk or clerical assistant should be defined by the librarian and these duties should be explicit. If there is more than one clerical assistant in the library, the librarian should designate duties for each, providing no overlapping of authority. Each position should carry a different salary and, as a result, each person should be motivated to do his job well.

Clerks and secretaries should have the minimum of a high school education. If the elementary school library is large enough, the secretary should have had secretarial training and/or experience and should be paid on the regular school salary scale for secretaries. This person must be willing and able to follow instructions carefully, and be open to suggestions for revitalizing routines which are often boring. Both the clerical and secretarial staff should have a pleasant voice, neat appearance, and a desire to serve students.

Both the clerical assistant and secretarial assistant should as-

---

[3] American Association of School Librarians, *Op. Cit.,* p. 58-59.

[4] American Library Association, *Loc. Cit.,* p. 16.

sist the librarian in the more obvious clerical tasks. Some of the duties which can further be assigned to these assistants are to assist the librarian in preparing reports and bibliographies, assist in the ordering and processing of library materials, and supervise the shelving and filing of library materials.

## STUDENT ASSISTANTS

The student assistant may be paid an hourly wage, or student assistance may be provided through involvement of the students in a student assistant library program. In the case of volunteer student assistance, the library representatives from each school room should provide much of the leadership. By working closely with these representatives, the librarian can involve the entire student body in library training. If the student assistant serves the library on a pay basis, then specific duties as well as hours of work should be arranged by the librarian. The paid student should be made to feel that he is an employee of the library and his behavior and library attitude should reflect the professional dignity of the position.

A student assistant library program should have the endorsement of the school administration. A policy-making session should be held with the school principal to establish guidelines for the student assistant program. Both the qualifications and duties of the assistant and the scheduling involved in setting up the program should have the principal's approval. The basic ideas for establishing a student assistant program, as contained in the guidelines recommended by the American Association of School Librarians, are to perfect a student's library skills and to develop desirable personal qualities in each student. In no instance should the work of the student library assistants become a substitute for the services of a professional librarian or paid clerical workers.[5]

There are various ways of selecting students who will be working directly with the librarian. A letter of application can be required from interested students, stating why they would like to be a library assistant and their qualifications. The teacher and principal should be consulted concerning those students they feel would be capable and dependable, but the final decision of selecting library assistants should rest with the librarian.

[5] American Association of School Librarians, *Op. Cit.*, pp. 20-21: 58.

There is no real reason why any student should be denied the role of library assistant. Regardless of grades, conduct, or physical and mental handicaps, there are services he can perform in the library. Quite often the rowdy child can develop self-control through library assistant work. Qualifications generally used in selecting library assistants are citizenship, dependability, friendliness, respect for others, initiative, and desire to work in the library.

If the student assistant program is an hourly pay program, the librarian should arrange a steady work schedule for the student. Such work should not infringe upon the regular school day. This means that students in the program must work before school, during lunch, and after school or during evenings and weekends. If the volunteer student assistant program is used, then students could be used during the school day. A program of this kind combines work with individual library instruction, and requires full cooperation from the teachers as well as students.

## VOLUNTEER ASSISTANCE OTHER THAN STUDENTS

Since 1958 there has been an accelerated use of volunteers in the elementary school library. The conscientious elementary librarian, as well as the school administrator, will want to consider the use of volunteers in the school library. Currently, the demand for library services outweighs the supply from the standpoint of not having as many librarians as are needed, and from the standpoint of school budgets not being large enough to pay salaries of needed personnel. Even in school libraries where personnel is plentiful, though, there are uses for volunteer helpers. To guarantee the development of quality volunteer assistants, the purposes of the volunteer program should be clearly outlined. Before any volunteer is accepted, he should complete a volunteer training program which includes study units in the various areas of library work.

Any program of volunteer assistance must be a cooperative endeavor receiving full support from all librarians and the school administrators. A program under any other conditions will not succeed.

# V

# ADMINISTRATIVE ORGANIZATION OF ELEMENTARY SCHOOL LIBRARIES

The administration of organized or semi-organized libraries in elementary schools has been accepted as the job for a professionally trained school librarian. There are basically three types of administrative organization in use today: administration by the Board of Education, administration by the public library, and administration through a multi-system of libraries.

## Administration by the Board of Education

Approximately 93 percent of the libraries in the United States are controlled directly by Boards of Education.[1] Administration by the Board of Education can take three forms: direct control, delegated administrative control and delegated supervisory control.

DIRECT CONTROL. Under this type of control, the Board of Education hires the librarian for each library. The difficulty with this plan is that the librarian is directly responsible to the Board of Education and he can function independently of the school which he serves. A great deal of friction can develop over the fact that the librarian can by-pass the principal on library affairs of an administrative nature.

DELEGATED ADMINISTRATIVE CONTROL. In this type of control the school administrator has the responsibility of carrying out the program of the Board of Education. He is vested with the authority to develop an educational program for the school. Thus, each school administrator employs a librarian to administer the school's library program. Under this system, there is the

---

[1] U. S. Office of Education, *Statistics of Public School Libraries,* Washington: GPO, 1968.

possibility of very little coordination among schools in the same school district.

DELEGATED SUPERVISORY CONTROL. The best type of administrative control by the Board of Education is through a school district library supervisor. The district library supervisor is accepted as the most functional type of administrative control as lines of authority are clear cut. The school district library supervisor should be a professionally trained and experienced librarian and is the supervisor for school library development within the district. This supervisor is on the screening board that employs new librarians and retains old ones. He is also on the curriculum committee concerned with making policies for curriculum development in the school district. In this role, he maintains close contact with the state school library supervisor so the district will be aware of state trends in relation to local needs. In effect, the supervisor shapes library development within the district to meet the needs of the administration, students and teachers from grades K-12.

## Administration by the Public Library

This type of control occurs when the Board of Education delegates either complete or partial control over school libraries to the public library. Normally, the public library board selects the school library supervisor who then selects his own staff for the schools. Quite often, the person selected by the public library to perform the duties of school library coordinator is the children's librarian or chief of the school department of the public library.

The method of control under these agreements varies widely. The agreement may include financial support of the librarian and/or financial support for equipment, supplies and library materials. Under an agreement of this type, every item concerned with the administration of the school library program should be stipulated in the contract to avoid possible misunderstanding. Although there are some examples of programs administered through a public library-school board cooperative agreement, local and state governmental agencies are usually so complicated that an agreement of this nature is awkward and less effective than control by the Board of Education.

Boards of Education can make short term contracts with public library boards for special services, such as acquisition and processing of library materials, and supervisory and consultant services. Contractual relations of this type are recommended and can serve as the basis of more general cooperative arrangements among various libraries of the area.

## Administration of School Libraries Through a Multi-System

The problems in financing desired levels of library service are today generally known. Even in many of the large city school systems, funds are not available for the establishment of libraries in each school. Further, in rural areas and small towns funds are even less available for needed personnel and library services. At one time, small schools depended to a large degree upon their county or public library. This, however, was not an effective means of providing quality library service. Today small schools, either within a school district or within an entire county, can make use of the multi-system of library organization.

Some advantages to this type of administrative organization are: central processing and acquisition, uniformity of cataloging and organizational structure, and inter-library cooperation in lending and acquisition.

Two types of administrative organization commonly practiced are the multi-county approach and the county-wide approach. Under the multi-county organization a number of adjoining counties agree to employ a director who will implement library service to all schools in these counties. The director hires an administrative staff, purchases a central collection of books and library material, provides scheduled delivery and pickup of library material, and provides demonstrations on their use. The multi-county approach usually implements a central catalog of holdings in all schools so that other schools in the multi-county area can utilize all the materials within the area.

Many counties have populations of less than 20,000 and no towns with more than 3,000 population. In such counties, the county-wide school library agreement is a recommended form of administrative organization. By having a central library to serve the entire county, professional librarians can be employed to administer library services. A central county system of school libraries would mean a huge central library, with deliveries of book collections to the various schools in the county. The administrator in each school would appoint a person to administer the book collection within the school, preferably a librarian. Under this arrangement, the school could use money otherwise spent on books to pay the salary of the librarian. The librarian or person administering the collection of books on loan from the central county library would determine needs from teachers, make requests for materials from the county center, and have books and various instructional materials for school use available at all times. Such a school library would not require as much space as a library recommended by the American Library Association, but it would provide a method of supplying books and badly needed instructional materials to children and teachers.

# VI

# ADMINISTRATION OF TECHNICAL PROCESSES

The technical processes in a school library involve selection, acquisition, cataloging, processing, and the repairing and binding of books. These functions are the backbone of the library and are performed under the direction of the librarian.

Every school needs a collection of well selected and up-to-date books in all subject areas. A wide range of reference books should supplement the general book collection. A variety of reading levels should be represented to satisfy the non-reader as well as the advanced student in each grade.

## SELECTION OF LIBRARY MATERIALS

In choosing materials for a school library, the librarian must have an understanding of the school's curriculum, a knowledge of the new books available, and a knowledge of the library's present collection. Selection of materials for a school library is a cooperative endeavor among the administration, faculty, students, and librarian. A selection committee, headed by the librarian and made up of faculty and a representative from the administration, should meet monthly or more often to decide purchases for the library. Orders for materials should be made immediately after the meeting of the selection committee.

Teachers and students should be urged to submit recommendations for materials to the committee. A simple request form should be provided by the librarian to all teachers and also should be available to the students. (Cf. Illustration No. 2) The librarian should keep the library collection balanced according to the objectives and the needs of the school. It is the librarian's responsibility to fill the gaps of the collection both in subject areas and reading levels.

| Class No. | AUTHOR (Surname first) | | |
|---|---|---|---|
| Accession No. | TITLE | | |
| No. of Copies Ordered | | | |
| Date Ordered | Place and Publisher | | Year |
| From | Edition or Series | Volumes | List Price |
| Date Received | Illustrator | | No. of Copies |
| Cost | Dept. for which Recommended | | Reviewed In |
| L.C. or Wilson Card | Teacher making Request | | DEMCO 18-263 |

*Illustration No. 2. Library Request Form.*

When ordering materials for the school library collection, the librarian needs the support of the school board and administration. This is essential since all factions and groups within the community and school can never be in complete agreement on all materials to be placed in the school library. One method of obtaining administrative support is to familiarize the Board of Education and administrators with the School Library Bill of Rights.[1] Some librarians keep a copy of the "Bill of Rights" on their desk at all times for ready reference. The library should also have a clearly established selection policy setting forth the school's principles for selection of library materials. Such a policy should be written and endorsed by the school board, the administration and the faculty. A written policy would include the following: (1) A statement of policy stating that the governing body of the school is legally responsible for all matters relating to the operation of the library. If authority is delegated, such delegation should be stated in the policy. (2) A statement indicating that materials for the school library should be selected by professional personnel in consultation with administration, faculty, students and parents and that final decisions for all purchases should rest with the librarian. (3) Book selection criteria which cover all types

[1] American Association of School Librarians, *Standards for School Library Programs.* Chicago: ALA, 1960, p. 75.

of materials that might possibly be selected for the school library. (4) Objectives of selection that are based upon the purposes and objectives of the library and school. (5) Procedures for consideration of criticism of materials in the school library.

The selection of library materials is a continuous process. The librarian must constantly check lists of materials in current selection aids as well as noting older items that should be added to the collection. The following list identifies some aids that help in the selection of books for the elementary school library: *Children's Catalog, Junior High School Collection, Elementary School Library Collection, Basic Book Collection for Junior High Schools, Library Journal, Wilson Library Bulletin, Bulletin of the Center for Children's Books, Horn Book, Grade Teacher,* and *Elementary English.*[2]

Publisher and jobber catalogs are also possible sources for selection. These catalogs are publications which should be critically examined. However, if one maintains a cautious approach and checks the validity of the description of the materials in one of the standard selection tools, the publisher and jobber catalogs can be valuable aids. Mail advertisements should also be checked against the standard selection tools before an order is placed. Materials on display at professional meetings provide an opportunity to comparatively evaluate some books. Another good source of ideas for orders is to browse through the collections of neighboring libraries and select the materials that would be of value to your collection.

Books on an award list should not be ordered automatically unless the book can be of use to your students and faculty. This would also be true of ordering all books in a given series, particularly if the library has a limited budget. Further, publishers and jobbers should not be asked to select books for a library. The jobber or publisher cannot know what resources are in the library or its specific needs. Do your own selection. The more restricted your budget, the more carefully one must select materials for the library.

General criteria for the selection of both fiction and nonfiction are physical appearance, durability of binding and paper, harmony of text and illustrations, and quality of writing. Specific criteria for the selection of fiction are accuracy of setting, credibility of story as well as character and thematic development, style, and illustration. Specific criteria for the selection of non-fiction are accuracy, nature

---

[2] Bibliographical information on these sources can be found in the Bibliography of this book.

of illustration, presentation and author's reputation.

Weeding a collection is just as important as selection. The same basic principles of selection should be applied in weeding. When adding new materials to the collection, materials no longer needed should be removed. This procedure keeps the library collection useful and up-to-date. Like selection, weeding is a continuous process which must be done consistently.

## ACQUISITIONS

The exact methods by which books are acquired for a school library vary from one library to another. The important part of a library's acquisitions program lies in its organization. A program should be organized so that routines are defined and responsibilities delegated. The acquisitions program should include policies and routines which determine the allocation of the budget, the frequency of purchases, the procedures for searching, and the procedures for placing and receiving orders.

### Budget

The elementary school library budget should be allotted either by department within the elementary school (science, language arts, etc.) or by grade level. Normally, grade level is most common in actual practice, for in this way each teacher can feel a responsibility for selecting books. If the budget is allotted by department, the department head should exert the initiative in book selection and expenditure of the funds for his department.

### Frequency of Orders

Library acquisitions should be made throughout the school year. By acquiring books and materials continuously, they should arrive in the same manner. This will greatly facilitate processing by allowing an even work flow to be maintained.

### Searching Routines

After an item has been approved by the book selection committee, the librarian should search the item. Searching involves checking the request against the card catalog under both author and title to see if the item is already on order in the library, or if this is a new edition of an item already in the library. If the book is already in the library or on order, the request should be returned to the person originating it with a proper notation. If the book is to be ordered, then order information must be erified: author entry, title, publisher, date and price. Basic tools that should be used in this procedure are *Children's Catalog, Junior High School Catalog, Elementary School Library Collection, Library Journal,* and *Books in Print.* (See "Bibliography" for full information)

## Selecting the Vendor

Once the order information has been verified, the librarian should select the source from which the item will be purchased. If an order has been verified in *Books in Print,* the item can be ordered directly from the publisher. By ordering from the publisher, one has more bookkeeping but faster service is available; books may also be secured prior to publication. If the school does not care to order directly from the publisher, the librarian should select a jobber who can supply the majority of the books and library materials. The use of a jobber allows two advantages: the placement of a single order for books from a number of publishers and only one bill to pay; in addition, unusual billing requirements can also be worked out with a jobber. The major disadvantage with a jobber is that deliveries are often slower then if orders were placed directly with the publisher or the local book store.

The local book store offers the fastest service if the book is in stock. The librarian may also be able to take the material out on approval. Local book stores will probably set up exhibits for book fairs if pre-arranged, but on the other hand they may offer a smaller discount than either a jobber or the publisher. Securing books through the local book store also creates more bookkeeping unless billing is done at intervals rather than with individual purchases.

## Placing the Order

The request for library materials, having been verified as needed and currently available, should be transferred to a regular library purchase form. Formal purchase orders vary, but Illustration No. 3 features a typical multiple order form. The information from the formal request card should be typed in its proper place on the order. A five-copy multiple order form may be used in the following way: The first and second copy of the order should go to the vendor (the

34    THE ELEMENTARY SCHOOL LIBRARY

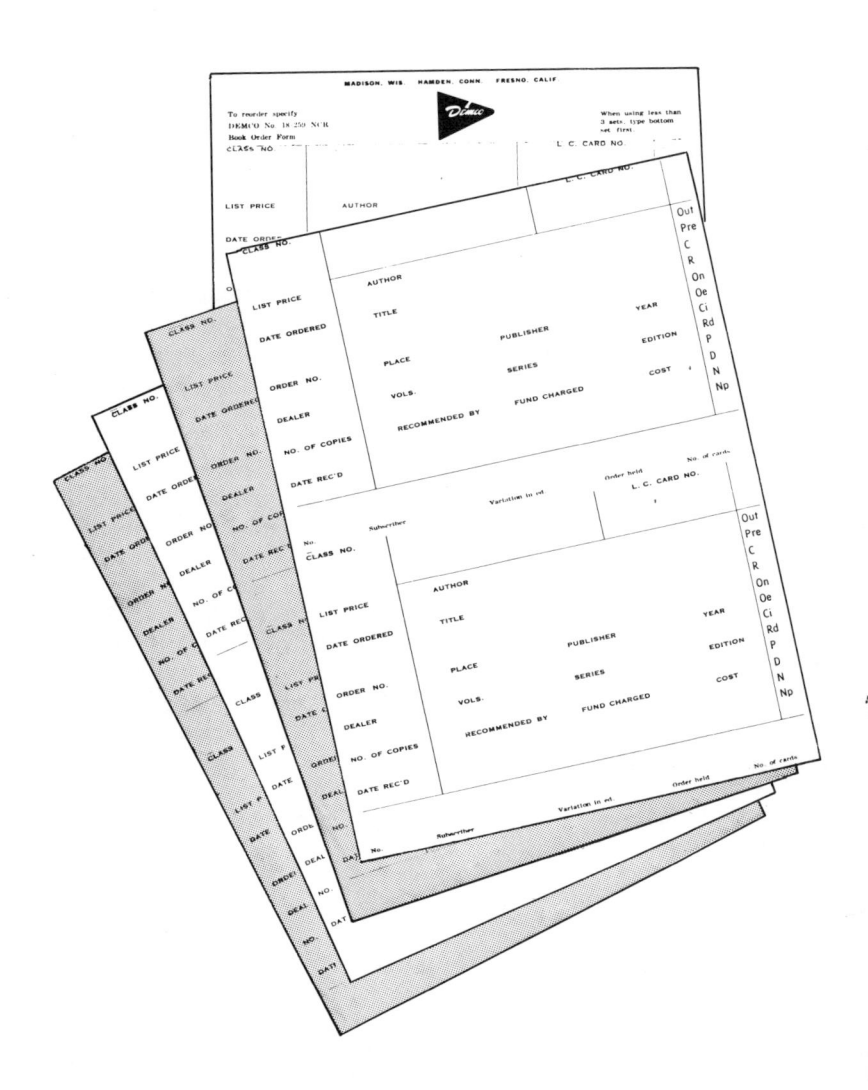

*Illustration No. 3. Multiple Order Form.*

second copy serves as a packing slip in shipment); the third copy should be filed in the "orders outstanding" file in the library workroom; the fourth copy should be used for ordering catalog cards; the fifth copy should be filed in the regular card catalog in the library reading area.

Some vendors will have a special order blank on which orders should be initiated; others may indicate that a letter will suffice. Regardless of the vendor's desires, the librarian should keep accurate order records and *all* ordering should be done in adherence with the basic regulations of the school district.

## Receipt of Shipment

When a shipment of library material arrives at the library, it should be carefully checked to insure accuracy. The vendor should have inserted the second copy of the book order in each book. The person opening the shipment should verify each packing slip against the item shipped. Each item should be checked for damage or imperfection. If the correct material was received in good order, then the matching order slip from the "orders outstanding" file in the library workroom should be pulled, dated, and inserted in the book with the packing slip.

If damaged or wrong merchandise is received, the librarian should not pull the order from the "orders outstanding" file; instead, a notation should be made as to status of the item (e.g., wrong title received and returned, 12-15-69) on the order record. Any damaged goods or receipt of wrong merchandise should be reported promptly to the vendor by letter; or, if volume of ordering is sufficient, a regular form letter should be devised for reporting deficient, damaged, and incorrect shipments.

The copy of the multiple order form returned as the packing slip and/or the vendor's packing slip should be sent to the school administrator's office in order that invoices can be cleared for payment. Those books meeting approval for payment should have the library ownership stamped in a conspicuous place (title page) and the accession number assigned to the book (stamped on bottom of first page after title page). The books are now ready for cataloging.

## CATALOGING AND PROCESSING

The librarian should have a separate work table or desk for the cataloging of library materials. Cataloging requires two basic tools: *Sears List of Subject Headings* and *Dewey Decimal Classification and Relative Index*. In addition, other aids are available to help one catalog books such as the *Children's Catalog, Junior High School Library Catalog,* and *Elementary School Library Collection.* (See "Bioliography" for full information) All of these provide complete catalog information, call number, subject headings and added entries. In general these aids provide all the information needed on the main entry card.

## Assigning the Call Number

The first step in cataloging involves the examination of the title page and copying all the pertinent information, i.e., author, title, publisher, place of publication, and date, on a work slip. The work slip should be a handwritten or typed slip of paper from which the final catalog cards will be typed. Verify the number of pages, illustrations and whether the book belongs to a series. Add this information to the work slip. Illustration No. 4 provides an example of the form of a work slip.

The second step in cataloging involves the examination of the

```
FIC
T969a   Twain, Mark
             The adventures of Tom Sawyer, by Samuel L.
        Clemens.   Illustrated by Norman Rockwell.   New
        York, Heritage Press, 1936.
             284 p.   illus.(part col.)   (The Heritage
        illustrated bookshelf)

             1. Missouri--Fiction.  2. Mississippi River--
        Fiction.   I. Rockwell, Norman, illus.  II. Title.
        (Series)
             x Clemens, Samuel Langhorne
```

*Illustration No. 4. Cataloging Workslip.*

book to determine its subject. Look at the title page to discover any clues as to the subject of the book. Further, refer to the original order source for information. Most of the sources used will have subject headings suggested for the book. Subjects may be determined in some books by the title or the subtitle. The preface or introduction might give a clue concerning the content of the book. The blurb on the book jacket should also be examined for possible clues to the subject. Bibliographies, indexes, chapter headings, and table of contents are other possible sources for determining the subject. If one still doubts that the right subjects have been chosen after considering the above items, then parts of the chapters should be read to determine the subject. If none of the above prove successful, consult a teacher in the school system that may have knowledge of the subject.

After the subject of the book has been determined, the *Dewey Decimal Classification and Relative Index*[3] should be consulted for determining classification numbers for all books other than fiction and biography. The introduction should be read slowly. If the librarian has used Dewey, he can then go directly to the tables to find the appropriate number that corresponds to the subject of the book. If the librarian is unfamiliar with Dewey, then the indirect approach is recommended; consult the index under the subject of the book for an indication as to the appropriate classification number. In using either approach, take special care to read all the notes that correspond to the correct number. Most school libraries should keep their call numbers to one or two decimals.

The second line of the call number can be established by taking the first three letters of the author's name. The number of *Birds in America* by John James Audubon is $\frac{598.2}{AUD}$ . Another source of the author line, and the one recommended, is the "Cutter" number.[4] This can be either a two or three digit number devised to correspond to the author's last name. Therefore, the book by Audubon, using the three digit "Cutter" number would be $\frac{598.2}{A897b}$ . The small "b" after the "Cutter" number stands for the title of the book.

It is recommended that all books in the school library be classified by the Dewey decimal classification scheme except fiction and

---

[3] Melvil Dewey, *Dewey Decimal Classification and Relative Index,* 9th abridged ed. Lake Placid, N.Y.: Forest Press, 1965.

[4] Charles A. Cutter, *Alphabetic Order Table Altered and Fitted with Three Figures,* by Kate E. Sanborn. Chicopee Falls, Mass.: H. R. Huntting Co., [n.d.]

biography. However, some librarians will find themselves in situations where various systems are in use. Some libraries have a combination of abbreviated Dewey numbers and symbols, others have only symbols. It is recommended that symbols be used for fiction and biography. Fiction should carry the symbol FIC with the second line of the call number being a "Cutter" number. E is recommended for picture books or easy books. BIO is recommended for biography. Biographies and easy books should also use the "Cutter" number for the second line of the call number.

## Assigning Subject Headings

*Sears List of Subject Headings*[5] should be consulted for the subject heading that best corresponds to the book. The introduction should be carefully read in order that this important tool can be utilized efficiently. Subject headings should be added to the work slip as indicated in Illustration No. 4, and any other tracings such as joint author, editor, illustrator, translator, organization, and title should be listed only in so far as deemed necessary. The work slip and book are now ready to move down the assembly line to the typist.

## Preparation of Catalog Cards

Catalog cards should be prepared for the public catalog in the library reading area and the shelf list. The typist should prepare a full set of catalog cards for the public catalog; the full set should consist of a main entry card, one card for each tracing at the bottom of the main entry, and a shelf list card. (See Illustration No. 5 for an explanation of main entry components.) Each tracing should be added to the top of a unit card, the unit card being an exact copy of the main entry card through the collation. Subject headings should be typed in black using all upper case letters. Title, illustrator, editor, joint author, translator, and compiler should be typed in black letters using both upper and lower case letters. The shelf list cards should be an exact copy of the main entry card with the accession number of the book typed in the lower left corner. Illustration No. 6 provides an example of a full set of typed catalog cards.

It is recommended that a librarian keep a shelf list rather than the traditional accession book record and that the shelf list be pub-

---

[5] Minnie E. Sears, *Sears List of Subject Headings,* 9th ed. New York: H. W. Wilson Co., 1965.

# ADMINISTRATION OF TECHNICAL PROCESSES 39

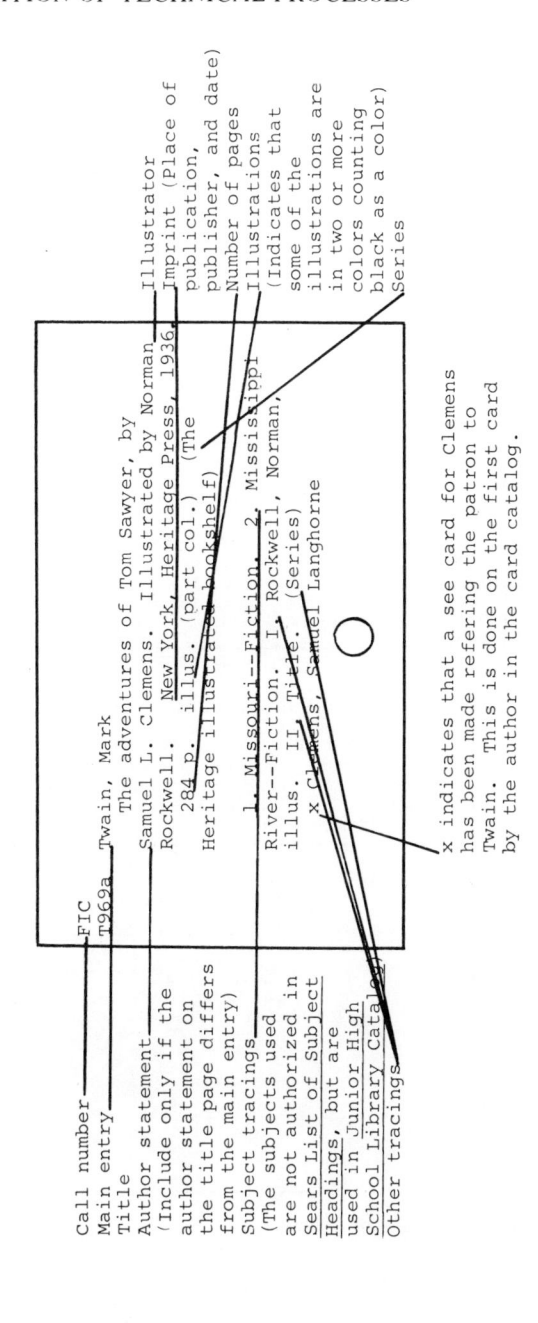

```
Call number ───── FIC
Main entry ───── T969a  Twain, Mark
Title ─────              The adventures of Tom Sawyer, by
Author statement          Samuel L. Clemens. Illustrated by Norman ───── Illustrator
(Include only if the      Rockwell.  New York, Heritage Press, 1936 ───── Imprint (Place of
author statement on       284 p.  illus. (part col.)  (The                publication,
the title page differs    Heritage illustrated bookshelf)                 publisher, and date)
from the main entry)                                                ───── Number of pages
Subject tracings ─────                                              ───── Illustrations
(The subjects used              1. Missouri—Fiction. 2. Mississippi       (Indicates that
are not authorized in        River—Fiction. I. Rockwell, Norman,          some of the
Sears List of Subject        illus. II. Title. (Series)                   illustrations are
Headings, but are               x Clemens, Samuel Langhorne               in two or more
used in Junior High                                                       colors counting
School Library Catalog)                                                   black as a color)
Other tracings ─────                                                ───── Series

                        x indicates that a see card for Clemens
                        has been made refering the patron to
                        Twain. This is done on the first card
                        by the author in the card catalog.
```

*Illustration No. 5. Main Entry Diagram.*

```
FIC
T969a    Twain, Mark
             The adventures of Tom Sawyer, by Samuel L.
         Clemens. Illustrated by Norman Rockwell.  New
         York, Heritage Press, 1936.
             284 p. illus.(part col.)  (The Heritage
         illustrated bookshelf)

             1. Missouri--Fiction. 2. Mississippi River--
         Fiction. I. Rockwell, Norman, illus. II. Title.
         (Series)
             x Clemens, Samuel Langhorne
```

```
FIC         MISSISSIPPI RIVER--FICTION
T969a    Twain, Mark
             The adventures of Tom Sawyer, by Samuel L.
         Clemens. Illustrated by Norman Rockwell.  New
         York, Heritage Press, 1936.
             284 p. illus.(part col.)  (The Heritage
         illustrated bookshelf)
```

```
FIC         MISSOURI--FICTION
T969a    Twain, Mark
             The adventures of Tom Sawyer, by Samuel L.
         Clemens. Illustrated by Norman Rockwell.  New
         York, Heritage Press, 1936.
             284 p. illus.(part col.)  (The Heritage
         illustrated bookshelf)
```

```
FIC         Rockwell, Norman, illus.
T969a    Twain, Mark
             The adventures of Tom Sawyer, by Samuel L.
         Clemens. Illustrated by Norman Rockwell.  New
         York, Heritage Press, 1936.
             284 p. illus.(part col.)  (The Heritage
         illustrated bookshelf)
```

*Illustration No. 6. Set of Typed Catalog Cards.*

# ADMINISTRATION OF TECHNICAL PROCESSES 41

```
FIC      The adventures of Tom Sawyer
T969a    Twain, Mark
            The adventures of Tom Sawyer, by Samuel L.
         Clemens. Illustrated by Norman Rockwell.  New
         York, Heritage Press, 1936.
            284 p. illus.(part col.)  (The Heritage
         illustrated bookshelf)
```

```
FIC      The Heritage illustrated bookshelf
T969a    Twain, Mark
            The adventures of Tom Sawyer, by Samuel L.
         Clemens. Illustrated by Norman Rockwell.  New
         York, Heritage Press, 1936.
            284 p. illus.(part col.)  (The Heritage
         illustrated bookshelf)
```

```
FIC
T969a       Twain, Mark
               The adventures of Tom Sawyer, by Samuel L.
            Clemens. Illustrated by Norman Rockwell.  New
            York, Heritage Press, 1936.
               284 p.  illus.(part col.)  (The Heritage
5387        illustrated bookshelf)
5388
5926           1. Missouri--Fiction. 2. Mississippi River--
            Fiction. I. Rockwell, Norman, illus. II. Title.
            (Series)
```

lic and available for student and teacher use. The shelf list provides a numerical listing by call number of all the materials in the library, the number of copies of a book, and an indication if the book has been withdrawn or lost. Further, the shelf list provides a duplicate of the main entry card in the event the main entry becomes lost.

## Preparation of the Book

The next step in processing involves the preparation of the book card and book pocket. The book pocket should be typed with call number and accession number; the book card should carry call number, acession number, author and title. The pocket should be affixed to the inside back cover of book and a date due slip affixed to the end paper facing the pocket. The book card should be inserted in the pocket. Examples of typed pocket, book card and date due slip are provided in Illustration No. 7.

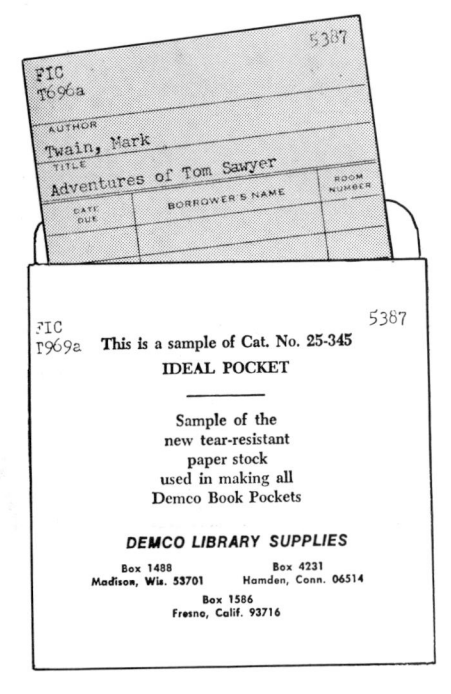

*Illustration No. 7. Typed Pocket, Book Card, Date Due Slip.*

ADMINISTRATION OF TECHNICAL PROCESSES                                43

The final step in processing the book consists of labeling the spine. Preferably, the labeling should be done by typing a cloth label in primary letters, then affixing the label to the spine approximately ½ inch from the bottom of the book. Pregummed labels should be purchased that are large enough to accomodate any call number. All cards, as well as pocket, book card and spine label should be checked for accuracy before the book and cards leave the workroom.

## Processing with Kits

Printed catalog cards are available as well as fully processed book kits. If the librarian had ordered the printed card kit, the kit should contain a full set of catalog cards. If the preprocessed book kit had been ordered, it should contain a full set of catalog cards, a book pocket, book card, date due slip, and a call number label for the spine of the book. Some firms also completely process books with book pocket and date due slip glued in the book, the spine labeled and the book jacket completely encased in a plastic book cover and attached to the book. With this type of processed book packet, the book is ready to be shelved when received, and the catalog cards are ready to be filed. The companies supplying these services can be found in the advertisements of professional journals. In addition, a list appears in the *Bowker Annual.*[6] The charge for these services varies, but the librarian should bear in mind that regardless of how good the pre-processed book kits seem, normally cataloging adjustments will have to be made in the cards, the call numbers and the subject headings.

## FILING

The filing of catalog cards in the main catalog should be kept as simple as possible. Children will be the primary users of the card catalog and it should not be complicated. A divided card catalog is recommended: One part should contain subject entries only, while the other part should contain main entries and added entries. This procedure enables a child to locate materials on a particular subject more easily since children primarily seek materials by subject in a card catalog.

Catalog drawers should be loosely filled, no more than three-fourths full at any time. A generous number of guide cards should

---

[6] *Bowker Annual of Library and Book Trade Information,* New York: R. R. Bowker Company, 1969.

be used in the card catalog and easy-to-read labels should be on the front of each drawer. Keep the card catalog up-to-date so that new materials may be easily located. The wise librarian will set some time aside each week for filing and revising activities. Separate the cards by subject and main/added entries. Alphabetize both of these groups before starting the filing.

Subject cards should be filed in a straight alphabetical arrangement, word by word, disregarding all punctuation.[7] If in doubt as to the manner the cards should be arranged, consult the arrangement of *Sears List of Subject Headings*. Until a person is skilled in filing, the librarian should always revise the work. If checking can be done immediately, the assistant should file above the rod in the card catalog drawer. If there should be a delay in the revising, the cards should be filed with a colored card behind them. The rod should then be pulled and all cards dropped and the rod replaced. When the librarian checks the filing, the colored cards are removed.

Filing of the main entry and added entry cards should also follow a straight alphabetical arrangement. At the time the main entry is filed, the order slip should be pulled and destroyed. Inter-file both primary and secondary entries. Works by a person (primary) and also works for which a person is the joint author, editor, illustrator, or compiler (secondary) should be inter-filed alphabetically by title.

The shelf list should be composed of two divisions; Dewey numbers and then symbols. The 000's-999's should be filed numerically, then alphabetically by the second line of the call number. The symbols should be arranged in alphabetical order. Within each symbol category cards should be arranged by the second line of the call number.

## INVENTORY

The librarian should conduct an inventory of the library collection yearly. Normally, this procedure cannot be carried on during the time when students and teachers are making use of the library's materials. Therefore, the inventory should be done during vacations or during the summer. Inventory consists of finding every item listed on the shelf list. As long as the librarian has a record of the location of an item, it should be counted as being available. If the librarian cannot locate an item, then it should be indicated as missing on

[7] See Appendix IV for an arrangement of filing.

the shelf list by its accession number. A note such as "mg.3/69" is sufficient. At the time an item becomes missing, the librarian must decide if the item should be replaced immediately or if a waiting period of one year is warranted. Normally, a waiting period of one year is recommended as quite often items return to the library within that period. If the librarian decides that an item should be withdrawn from the library, the following procedure should be followed: If there is more than one copy of the item on the shelf list, then merely mark a red line through the withdrawn item and indicate "wd.3/69." If the only copy of an item were being withdrawn, the card should be removed from the shelf list, and all the cards in the card catalog should be removed. All the cards are then destroyed.

## REPAIRING AND BINDING OF BOOKS

In the course of inventory, the librarian will discover books in need of repair or rebinding, and even books which should be discarded. Minor repairs should be supervised by the librarian, such as a torn page, a slit cover, or a torn spine. Supplies for mending books as well as a booklet on how to repair a book are available from most library supply companies.

Books that should be sent to a professional bindery include those that have loose or broken stitching of signatures, dog-eared and worn out covers, or a paperback book ready for permanent encasement. If a book has too many structural defects, such as brittle pages, narrow margins and poor print, then it should be discarded and a replacement copy or a substitute title should be ordered.

# VII

# ORGANIZATION OF PUBLIC SERVICES IN THE ELEMENTARY SCHOOL LIBRARY

The school librarian must be adept not only in organizing the technical services of the library but he must also be able to coordinate programs for the use of the public he serves. The public to the school librarian is composed of students, teachers, administrators, and the school community. The services of the library must be comprehensive and coordinated in such a way so that they can be administered in the least amount of time. Where technical services are normally in the background, the services rendered by the librarian to people are always seen and are the services by which the library is judged as to whether it is a good and a functional school library. In the organization of public services for the school library, the two large areas of organizational structure are the circulation system and general services to school and community.

## CIRCULATION

The librarian should design a circulation system for student and teacher use of all materials and resources of the library. The primary purpose of the circulation system should be to facilitate use of all library materials, at home and in school. In accomplishing this purpose, the librarian must provide for the widest possible use of library materials, make the proper adjustments between reference demands, home use and classroom use, and see that students have access to the library materials throughout the school year. Through the instructional program and reading guidance the librarian must be able to recognize need and connect the need to the right resource.

There are basically two types of circulation systems in use in school libraries. One is the "permissive type," or completely free

## ORGANIZATION OF PUBLIC SERVICES IN SCHOOL LIBRARY  47

circulation of all materials in the library. The other is the "non-permissive type" which is restrictive in whatever ways the librarian and the administration determines. The librarian coming into the new school library can be very influential in determining the type of circulation program to be utilized. If the library has been in operation for some years, the school will have already decided upon certain basic fundamentals in the circulation of library materials. An alert librarian, however, will always develop the best type of circulation system for that particular school library. If there are several school libraries within the school district, all circulation systems in the district should be the same.

The principle involved in the permissive circulation program is that of free circulation of all library materials to all students and teachers. The theory behind this principle is that library materials are purchased for use and that restriction of the circulation and use of any piece of library material violates the school's philosophy. A non-permissive circulation system is one which limits the free circulation of library materials to students and teachers. The only reason a school system might justify the use of a non-permissive circulation system is that the library collection is too small to provide library materials for all of its users.

In developing a circulation program for the school library, the librarian and school administrator should establish a policy governing the circulation program. This policy should include provisions for the use of library material, the type of circulation system, and recommended circulation procedures. It is suggested that all materials be loaned for home use to students and teachers, and that the duration of the loan be determined by the type and quantity of material.

An automatic charging machine is recommended for school libraries which circulate 300 or more items daily. These charging machines are available from several firms and prices vary according to the functions the machines perform. If a library's circulation is less than 300 items a day, a manual circulation system is recommended.

Certain basic equipment is needed for the circulation of library material, regardless of whether a manual or automatic charging system is used. A standard circulation desk is essential to facilitate the charge and discharge of library materials. Circulation desks which provide charging trays, supply drawers, a book return slot, shelves, a circulation file, and guide cards for separating cards, are available from many library furniture firms.

The actual process of circulation with a manual system consists of the borrower signing the book card with his name and room number and the desk attendant stamping the "date due" on the book card and the slip in the book. The attendant should then file by classification number. At the end of the day, circulation should be counted and recorded. Filing by classification numbers permits library employees and students to determine the location of an item merely by checking under its call number in the circulation file.

A reader's record should be kept at the circulation desk, unless circulation exceeds 300 items per day. Each child should be responsible for completing his reader's record. If circulation is greater than 300 items per day, the classroom teacher should be asked to encourage the students to keep their reader's record current in the classroom.

Periods of loan for the various library materials should vary according to the type and quantity of material. Normally, books should circulate for a period of two weeks, subject to being renewed upon request. If the patron still has not finished the book after the first renewal, the librarian should use his judgment in renewing the book. Reference books should circulate overnight, and should be borrowed the last period of the school day and returned during the first period of the next school day. Reference books should be allowed to be taken home again by the same student, if no one else has asked for the book. Multimedia (non-book) materials should follow the same general principles as regular library material.

Books may be placed on reserve if there is a great demand for them by students, or if teachers ask the librarian to place certain books on reserve. Books placed on reserve should be housed in special shelves behind the circulation desk and should normally be loaned for 2 hours or 3 days. Each book should be marked clearly as to length of loan and name of teacher for whom the book is on reserve. It is wise to keep a list of reserve books arranged alphabetically by teacher on the circulation desk for handy reference.

To discharge library loans, once library material has been returned to the library, the desk attendant should pull the matching book card from the circulation file, scratch through the borrower's name, insert the card in the book pocket, and mark through the "date due" on the slip in the book. The book is ready to be reshelved or circulated. The tardy return of books can sometimes be a problem for the librarian, but fines are not recommended in an elementary school library. The librarian, through other means, is encouraged to instill the important responsibility of returning library materials on time.

## SERVICES TO SCHOOL AND COMMUNITY

The second major area of public service for the school librarian consists of all those services the librarian provides to the school and community. To properly fulfill this important phase of library administration, the librarian should organize the services which he plans into services for students, teachers, school administrator and parents.

### Services to Students

In order to conduct an effective program of service to students, the librarian must seek the cooperation of the teachers within the school. In cooperation with the teachers, the librarian should plan weekly library periods in which book talks and story telling are used to increase the students' desire to read. The teacher and the librarian should be on the alert for students with reading difficulties from observations in the library and classroom, and consult with the reading specialist if necessary for proper corrective measures. A regular program of library instruction should be developed to assist all students in maximum library usage. The librarian and teacher can further cooperate through scheduling visitations to the public library through the librarian.

The librarian should plan activities that directly involve the students with the librarian. One of the more important of these activities is a program of directed reading and browsing in which the librarian can informally teach research methods and the principles of reading selection to students. The librarian can also organize a library club or an audio-visual club in which students can publish a library paper, prepare bibliographies, and assist in the use of audio-visual materials.

Each year the librarian should plan some activities that involve the entire student body. A "book fair," properly supervised, can be a very successful student project. The fair should be used as a technique for calling new books to the attention of the school community and not become simply a profit-making scheme.

## Services to Teachers

The librarian should cooperate with the teachers in his school in every possible way. One special service which the librarian can perform for the teachers should occur during the teachers' workshop preceding school. During this workshop period, the librarian should see that each teacher receives a copy of the library handbook in which services offered by the librarian may be found. In the workshop, the librarian should explain the purposes of the library. Impress upon the teachers that they are the official book selectors and encourage them to make recommendations for library acquisitions. A list of the library resources and cultural resources of the community should be distributed. Each teacher should be informed what resources are available in the school library in his area of interest. Further, the workshop is an excellent time to point out the facilities of the professional library.

As a follow-up to the workshop, the librarian should meet each teacher individually and identify any special services that he could perform for the teacher. Some of the services that the librarian could perform include instruction in use of the library, the offering of story hours, inter-library loans, and informing faculty and staff of new professional materials in the library.

## Services to the School Administrator

The school librarian is the director of the library program which the school administrator has approved. To fulfill this obligation, the librarian should be a promoter and develop a program of special services for the school administrator. Through a planned program, the librarian can effectively build a framework with which the administrator can expand the library's financial and physical limitations.

First, the administrator must be provided with information. The librarian should keep the administrator informed of library development on the state, national and local levels: advise him on any new standards for library programs which have been recommended by the State Department of Education. Let the administrator know how his school library compares with libraries in school districts of the same size within the state, and how the library ranks in comparison with other school districts in his county or parish. With a little research, the librarian can find that the library ranks in some aspects higher than surrounding libraries. At the same time, suggestions for improvement can be made. Secondly, the administrator often requires research on various topics from the librarian. If the librarian does not feel his research thoroughly answers the question posed by the administrator, he should suggest that this research be performed by a committee under the librarian's leadership. Third, the librarian should offer to work with the administrator on curriculum planning and serve on the curriculum planning committee, for by serving on it the librarian will be able to fulfill the library's objectives in the curriculum. Further, through service on the curriculum committee, the librarian can anticipate the supplementary types of library materials needed.

## Role of the Librarian in the Community

In addition to services to students, teachers and the administrator, the librarian should serve as liaison for the school in the community. A librarian does not consciously have to fulfill this role, it is an automatic result of working with the students, the teachers, and administrative personnel. A librarian does, however, have to exert effort to interpret the school library program to the community.

The school librarian must be able to interpret the school library in meaningful terms to parents. First, alert parents to the fact that there is a school library and a librarian. Students can do an excellent job of this by writing letters to their parents informing them what the library is and how it has best served them. After a student participation project, formal invitations to a library "open house" can be sent by the librarian to the parents of all the children in the school. It is suggested the "open house" be held during the same evening that the school is also holding "open house." At this time, the library should demonstrate that it is a place for and about children. Let the students be guides and also answer questions on how to use the library. The librarian can then be a roving ambassador visiting with everyone and explaining the library's facilities. During this visit, provide parents with a bibliography of books for children. An excellent way of demonstrating that the library is an integral part of the total school program is to secure the cooperation of teachers in preparing the bibliography which would contain leisure reading, hobbies, a list of classics, and children's selections (preferably graded) that parents might consider for a home library.

# VIII

# PHYSICAL FACILITIES

The school library should be planned by the librarian, the school administrator and the architect. The librarian knows the functions the library must perform, the school administrator knows the financial limitations, and the architect should be able to provide an adequate compromise.

For those librarians in less than the ideal situation, remodeled library facilities must be considered. Remodeling can range from adding an additional room to the existing library, or setting up a library in a vacated classroom, closet or corridor. Regardless of the situation, the librarian should know how to best utilize the available space.

There are certain basic principles one must consider in planning physical facilities for the school library. The size of the physical facility depends upon the enrollment, the curriculum, and the library services desired. A permanent library facility must also be planned in relation to the stability of the plant in which it is located. Ideally the library is centrally located on the first floor of the school, adjacent to classrooms and near the administrative offices, but away from music rooms, the gymnasium, the industrial arts shop and cafeteria. If use of the library after school is anticipated, an outside entrance is necessary so that the entire building will not have to be open. Restroom facilities should be near the library or within it, and the library planned so that future expansion is possible.

The general physical plant of the school building ought to provide heating and ventilation of the school library. Lighting should range between fifty and seventy foot candles, and acoustical adaptation of the floor covering (carpet, vinyl, tile, or cork) and ceiling tile is recommended. Windows should be placed so that shelving can be accommodated on each wall, and telephone outlets are suggested for both the office and workroom.

## RECOMMENDED AREAS OF THE LIBRARY

The physical areas recommended for the elementary school library are: main reading room, librarian's office, workroom, professional reading room, conference room, classroom, receiving and sorting room, periodical storage room, restroom, and audio-visual room. Illustration No. 8 indicates how these recommended areas should be physically related to each other and Illustration No. 9 provides a chart of furnishings by area.

## Reading Room

The reading room should have sufficient floor space to accommodate 15 percent of the school's enrollment, but not more than 100 students should be seated in any one area. If 15 percent of the school's enrollment is 100 students, another reading room should be provided within the library. If there are less than 350 students enrolled in the school, then the reading room should seat 50 students. Rectangular shaped areas are more adaptable to the placement of furnishings than areas of any other shape.

SHELVING. Types of shelving and color schemes should be coordinated throughout the library. For a basic collection of 10,000 books, 70 units of bracket type shelving (3' x 3'6") will be needed. Estimated on the basis of 15 volumes per linear foot, each unit will shelve 144-150 books. Ten percent of the 70 units will normally carry 10" wide shelves with the remainder 8" wide shelves. Some additional special shelving 12" deep with one-fourth inch upright partitions spaced 7 to 8 inches apart in each shelf is needed for picture books. A regular sized (72" x 72" x 12") magazine rack provides sufficient shelving for current periodicals, and a newspaper rack with 6 newspaper rods can accommodate current issues of newspapers.

TABLES AND CHAIRS. A school with an enrollment of 350 students should provide study tables (25" to 28" high) and chairs (14" to 17" high) for at least 50 students. It is recommended that 50 percent of the seating be individual study-type carrels. The remainder of the study spaces should consist of tables (4' to 5' diameter) to seat four to five readers. Cushions with washable coverings are recommended for storytelling purposes in the picture book area of the reading room.

CIRCULATION DESK. The circulation desk should be a standard three-module, U-shaped desk with entrances at both ends. The desk includes filing trays, shelves, and a book return slot compartment. Stools, one contoured chair, and two waste baskets should be purchased as supplementary items for the circulation desk.

CARD CATALOG. The card catalog should consist of two physical catalogs (6 trays x 5 trays) no higher than five feet. One catalog is to be used for the subject catalog; the other for main and added entries, and the shelf list.

BOOK TRUCKS. One book truck equipped with rubber tires and bumpers is needed in the library. If books are frequently taken to classrooms, additional book trucks are recommended.

VERTICAL FILE. The vertical file should consist of at least four file cabinets (48" x 18" x 15"). These cabinets should be with durable file guides and removable rods.

## Librarian's Office

The librarian's office is to be furnished with 4 file cabinets measuring 48" x 18" x 15", open book shelves (9' x 5' x 10'), and a special library typewriter. It should also have an intercommunications outlet to the main office and the library, and glass vision panels.

## Workroom

The workroom should contain a work-type cabinet with a formica covered counter, a sink (15" x 30" x 24"), and wall cupboards above the cabinet measuring 5' x 2½ ' x 20". The workroom should be arranged so that it allows an even flow of work to be maintained.

## Conference Room

The conference room should be equipped with overhead, indirect lighting, a 3' x 10' table (25" to 28" high), and 12 chairs (14" to 17" high). There should be a glass partition between the reading room and conference room so supervision is possible. Movable wall shelves 3 to 4 shelves high for special collections should be included as well as 16" wide shelving for recordings. A record player, movie projector, and filmstrip projector can be stored in the room for general use.

## Receiving and Sorting Room

The receiving and sorting room should have shelving sufficient to accommodate storage of shipments received. A two-wheeled dollie will be necessary to handle receipt and transfer of shipments. The receiving and sorting room can also be used for emergency storage of periodicals and books.

## Periodical Storage Room

The peridoical storage room should contain shelving on each wall. A glass partition, between the periodical storage room and reading room, is recommended.

## Professional Reading Room

The professional reading room should contain professional books and periodicals which assist teachers in classroom preparation and keep them abreast of new curriculum developments. The furnishings of this room should be informal in character, and include facilities for the production of teaching aids.

## Audio-Visual Room

The audio-visual room should be a functional part of the library's physical structure.[1] The storage facilities for multimedia in the audio-visual room should be adequate to accommodate all types of material. Films should be shelved on adjustable shelving with racks to hold film cans of all sizes. Tiers of wall cubicles can also be built in two sizes to hold different sizes of film cans. Storage for filmstrips should utilize shallow (1-3/4") drawer cabinets, 15" wide x 12" deep x 12" high (capacity: 300 cans). Recordings should be stored in cabinets fitted with shallow shelves to accommodate 12" recordings and 16" tape transcriptions. All recordings cabinets should be closed,

[1] A list of the basic equipment for an audio-visual center is provided in *Standards for School Media Programs*.

dust free, and provide for upright storage of recordings. Shelving 18" apart can be built for radios; playback machines and other equipment should be housed in cupboards of appropriate sizes, and carts used to house machinery that is transported to classrooms frequently. Maps and graphics should be stored in cabinets known as map storage cabinets in supply catalogs. The cabinets should be placed on bases at least 12" from the floor but not more than 30" in height.

## Other Areas

Other areas in the school which are sometimes considered part of the library plant are the language laboratories and various learning centers. Unless these are administered by the librarian, they should not be considered part of the library. If they are administered by the librarian, they must be coordinated as part of the overall library organization. Specifications for floor plans and furnishings for these two possible areas are provided by the Educational Facilities Laboratories in several different publications.[2]

Appendix V provides several floor plans to assist one in planning either a library remodeled from a classroom or a new plan for the most modern library. Even a small start of a central library in an old supply room is a big beginning. From such a beginning ideal situations can evolve through effective planning. In developing plans for libraries, one must not hesitate to consult the American Library Association as well as one's State Department of Education for advice.

[2] The address of Educational Facilities Laboratories, Inc., is 477 Madison Avenue, New York, N.Y.

# IX

# ORGANIZATION AND ADMINISTRATION OF MULTIMEDIA RESOURCES

Multimedia materials are essential in the fulfillment of the educational program of our schools. As late as 1960, the term audio-visual was in vogue and referred primarily to a few materials that were available. These materials were motion pictures, maps, pictures, models, graphs, and charts. Today, the modern term multimedia is used to describe all types of non-book media. Some of these are pictures, pamphlets, clippings, 3- dimensional objects, realia, globes, programmed textbooks, standardized tests, occupational guidance leaflets, teaching machines, reading pacers, and tape retrieval systems. No longer can one think of non-book teaching materials as being merely audio-visual aids.

Libraries began to heavily acquire multimedia resources after the passage of the National Defense Education Act of 1958 and the Elementary and Secondary Education Act of 1965. This legislation made funds available for the purchase of supplementary materials for schools and libraries. Also, through the financial impetus, some state departments of education prepared brochures and guidelines for processing multimedia resources, but few prepared guidelines for the evaluation and selection of multimedia resources. Multimedia resources, therefore, will be considered with respect to administration in the areas of selection, acquisition, and organization, as well as processing.

## SELECTION OF MULTIMEDIA MATERIALS

In the selection of multimedia resources, the same care and scrutiny is to be exercised that is exercised when purchasing a book. This means that before a purchase is made, the librarian and teacher should try to verify the quality of the items through actual examination or non-biased reviews of the items. For multimedia resources this is a big order. First of all, it is almost impossible for many librarians and teachers to actually examine the various multimedia resources that they may desire to purchase. Where publishing companies and private associations provide book exhibits, no such service is provided for multimedia materials. Presently, the closest one can come to having a mass preview of new equipment and materials is by attending the annual convention of the Division of Audio-Visual Instruction of the National Education Association. Thus, if a person desires to examine a piece of equipment, or a 3-dimensional object, or even preview a recording before purchase, special effort must be exerted to contact an area representative for the company which sells the item so that he can present the item for preview and examination purposes. Some companies will send examination copies of multimedia through the mail. Other companies supply preview sheets of the frames of a filmstrip or the contents of a set of posters; such preview may be obtained free of charge by the librarian. This service saves time in that the selection committee previews the whole filmstrip on a sheet of paper instead of setting up the filmstrip projector. Also this eliminates the necessity of sending the items back if not purchased by the librarian.

Since physical examination of each item recommended for purchase is not possible for all items, the only acceptable alternative is to investigate an item recommended for purchase through critical reviews in professional journals or multimedia and library tools. Some of the better and more practical sources for review of multimedia are: *Subscription Books Bulletin, A-V Instruction, Library Journal, Educational Media Index, Guide to Free Tapes, Transcription and Recordings,* and *National Tape Repository.*

The selection committee recommends the purchase of multimedia items, but final responsibility for the selection of multimedia rests with the librarian. The librarian should build a file of information that serves as a review source and also a file to justify his decision in selection.

## ACQUISITION OF MULTIMEDIA RESOURCES

The acquisition of multimedia resources must be based on the same principles involved in the acquisition of regular library material. The normal procedure consists of faculty, through use of the regular library request from, recommending that an item be acquired for the library. The librarian should verify the information and locate reviews of the material so that the committee can decide if the material should be purchased. Material may also be acquired free of charge; however, free material should undergo the same scrutiny as materials considered for purchase.

Although the purchase of multimedia resources is the most economical method of acquisition, there are situations in which other methods may be used. The librarian may decide that an item would better be leased than purchased. Lease of expensive equipment is quite common. Also, there is the lease-purchase arrangement which allows a school to apply the money invested in the lease toward purchase. Many multimedia materials, however, are better borrowed than bought. Borrowing material often allows the library to provide immediate service to teachers; further, if a library has a limited budget for curriculum enrichment materials, borrowing expensive materials can stretch the budget farther.

## CATALOGING AND PROCESSING MULTIMEDIA RESOURCES

The various multimedia resources must be organized, cataloged, and made available for easy use. They should be processed (cataloged, physically marked, date due slips attached, and catalog cards filed) according to the basic procedures established for books. In order to give organization to the various types of resources that might possibly be processed, the cataloging and processing procedures are divided by type of material treated.

### Newspapers and Magazines

All newspapers and magazines should be sent directly to the workroom for processing. If this is a new title for the library, a main entry card should be made for the regular card catalog in the library's reading area, the call number being the word "Periodical." Aside from the main entry, a periodical holdings card should be made. (See Illustration No. 10) The periodical holdings card contains the title of the periodical as given on the main entry card, the cost of the subscription, number of copies received, the record of issues received, the source of the periodical (agent/distributor), and subscription expiration date. Issues which have been discarded can also be indicated if desired. The periodical holdings card should be filed in the periodical holdings file in the workroom.

After recording the periodical on the holdings card, the front upper right corner should be stamped with the library's ownership. Current issues of magazines may be placed in plastic covers for protection. On some of the heavier magazines, a reinforcing strip of tape may be placed on the spine.

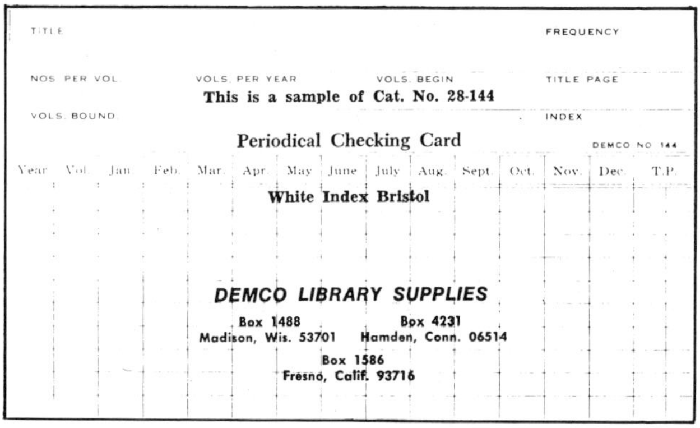
TITLE FREQUENCY
NOS. PER VOL. VOLS. PER YEAR VOLS. BEGIN TITLE PAGE
This is a sample of Cat. No. 28-144
VOLS. BOUND INDEX
Periodical Checking Card
DEMCO NO. 144
Year Vol. Jan. Feb. Mar. Apr. May June July Aug. Sept. Oct. Nov. Dec. T.P.
White Index Bristol
DEMCO LIBRARY SUPPLIES
Box 1488 Madison, Wis. 53701
Box 4231 Hamden, Conn. 06514
Box 1586 Fresno, Calif. 93716

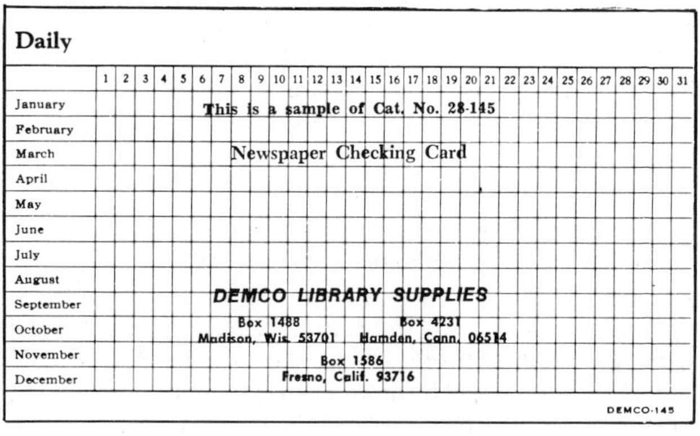
Daily
1 2 3 4 5 6 7 8 9 10 11 12 13 14 15 16 17 18 19 20 21 22 23 24 25 26 27 28 29 30 31
January
February
March
April
May
June
July
August
September
October
November
December
This is a sample of Cat. No. 28-145
Newspaper Checking Card
DEMCO LIBRARY SUPPLIES
Box 1488 Madison, Wis. 53701
Box 4231 Hamden, Conn. 06514
Box 1586 Fresno, Calif. 93716
DEMCO-145

*Illustration No. 10. Periodical Holdings Card.*

## Other Multimedia Resources

Other media because of their format are treated and housed separately. All receive the same type of cataloging and processing procedures. To catalog the various multimedia resources, assign an accession number beginning with number "1" for each type of media. The accession number preceded by the appropriate symbol for the material completes the call number. (Illustration No. 11 contains sample main entry cards for various multimedia) If there should be more than one copy of an item, indicate the number of copies on the shelf list, (425a, 425b, etc.). The call number in the upper left hand corner of the card indicates the kind of material and the accession number. The more common symbols used are listed below; however, with the many new types of materials being produced each year, the librarian will add to the list of symbols as needed.

| Symbol | Type of Media |
| --- | --- |
| R | Disc recordings |
| F | Films |
| FS | Filmstrips |
| GA | Games |
| G | Globes |
| GR | Graphics |
| K | Kits |
| M | Maps |
| MS | Models and Specimens |
| PT | Programmed texts |
| S | Slides |
| TR | Tape recordings |
| TRAN | Transparencies |
| VF | Vertical file |

The multimedia catalog cards should be inter-filed in the regular card catalog and shelf list; therefore, it is important to do full cataloging, making the proper cross references and subject headings.

```
FS
96        Introduction to the library.  Script by Owen T. P.
            McGowan.  Editorial supervision by John O'Shea
          Cadden.  New York, Eye Gate House, 1965.
            35 fr., 35 mm., col.  (Library research tools)

          Introduces the card catalog, shelf arrangement
          of books, magazines and newspapers, non-book
          materials, and vertical file materials.

            1. Library science.  (Series)
```

```
G
28        Weisgard, Leonard
            Mother Goose nursery pictures; decorative prints
          in full color.  New York, Penn Prints, 1957.
            6 prints, 13"x16", col.

            Contents.--Old Mother Hubbard.--Ride a cock
          horse.--Peter, Peter, Pumpkin Eater.--Three
          little kittens.--Little Boy Blue.--Little Bo
          Peep.

            1. Nursery rhymes--Pictures, illustrations, etc.
          I. Title.
```

```
K
19        Williams, John C
            Library skill kit II, by John C. Williams;
          with consultants James A Dennan and Robert A.
          Lodge.  Clark Summit, Penn., Logo Publishing and
          Research Co., 1967.
            90 lessons (approx.) on 8"x10" cards.

            With work sheets, answer keys, and teacher's
          guide.
            The introduction lesson to each section has 25
          cards.
                                                   (over)
```

*Illustration No. 11. Multimedia Main Entry Cards.*

# ORGANIZATION OF MULTIMEDIA RESOURCES

```
M
36     American Map Company, Inc.
         Colorprint general map of the World on
       Mercator's projection; featuring all political
       divisions, principal cities, and shortes steam-
       ship distances between ports.  New York, n.d.
         38"x50", col.

         Scale: 1"=500 miles.

         1. Earth--Maps.  I. Title.
```

```
R
52      Songs from Singing every day.  Boston, Ginn, n.d.
          10 s., 10", 78 rpm.  (Our singing world)

          Contents.--Playtime songs.--Just for fun.--
        Singing at work.--Singing games.--Home and family.
        --Music's makers.--Happy holidays.--Seasons.--
        Creatures great and small.--Singing things.
          To supplement the textbook entitled Singing
        every day, by Lilla Belle Bitts and others.

          1. Children's songs.  I. Title: Singing every
        day.  (Series)
```

```
TRAN
47       Instructo Corp.
           The brain.  Paoli, Penn., 1967.
           1 transparency, 5 overlaies, 10"x10", col.
         (The body, no. 818-13)

           With teaching guide.
           Illustrates the shape, appearance, location,
         major parts and functions of the brain.

           1. Brain.  (Series)
```

```
F
12      Know your library.    Chicago, Coronet, 1962.
           11 min., 16 mm., sd., col.

        An introduction to reference and the library.

        1. Libraries.
```

```
F
12      Know your library.    Chicago, Coronet, 1962.
           11 min., 16 mm., sd., col.

        An introduction to reference and the library.

        1. Libraries.
```

```
F       LIBRARIES
12      Know your library.    Chicago, Coronet, 1962.
           11 min., 16 mm., sd., col.
```

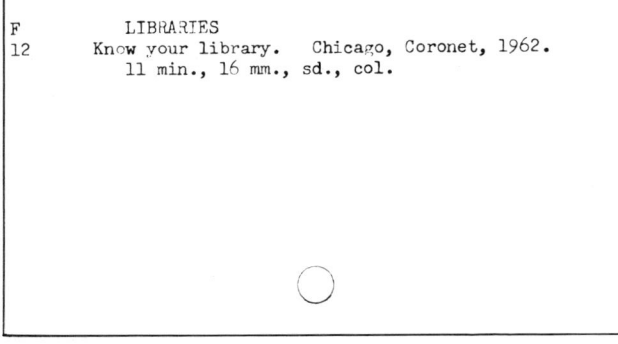

*Illustration No. 11. Multimedia Main Entry Cards.*

## PHYSICAL ORGANIZATION

In the elementary school, the school administrator will find it wise to coordinate the various instructional, curriculum and multimedia resources through the elementary school library. If the library is providing films, filmstrips, recordings, tapes, realia, pamphlets, pictures, and their servicing, then these materials must not only be cataloged as previously mentioned, but they must be arranged and housed in physical surroundings that make use of them easy and inviting.

### Newspapers and Magazines

Newspapers and magazines are to be kept in the main reading room of the library, preferably in a special corner of the room near the *Reader's Guide to Periodical Literature*. The current issues of newspapers should be displayed for use on regular newspaper rods, and current issues of magazines should be enclosed in plastic covers and displayed on a standard magazine rack. Back issues of newspapers and magazines can be kept nearby in a periodical storage area arranged by title on regular book shelves that are accessible to the students and faculty.

### Vertical File

Materials cataloged for the vertical file should be stored in regular legal size filing cabinets, two drawers in height. The files should be near the card catalog and reference area of the library. Drawers are to be clearly labeled and accessible for use throughout the school day.

### Other Multimedia Materials

Other multimedia materials because of their physical properties and their form require special storage facilities and services. Materials should be kept in call number order for ease in identification and use. Maps ought to be stored flat in regular map cases. Games, globes, graphics, kits, models and specimens should be stored in upright storage cabinets with adjustable shelves. Programmed textbooks should be shelved on regular book shelving in the reading room. Recordings, films, slides, tapes, transparencies, and filmstrips require not only special storage facilities but also special areas for use of the materials.

In schools with enrollments of 1,000 or fewer students, at least 200 square feet of floor space should be provided for small group viewing and listening. This space should exist in addition to the regular library conference rooms.[1] Wherever possible, the audio room ought to be separate from the viewing room. The walls and ceiling of both rooms should be sound proof. Humidity held at approximately 40% and temperature at 70° will assure optimum storage conditions. In the viewing areas, the lighting should be equipped with dimming switches.

Approximately 600 square feet are necessary for housing audio-visual materials in a centralized library facility. If the audio-visual room is not an integral part of the library, then extra space must be allowed for a viewing and listening area. Storage for audio-visual equipment and materials ought to be adjacent to the library's reading room and close to the viewing and listening room.[2] Storage facilities and equipment for furnishing the area can be found in the *Audio-Visual Equipment Directory*.[3]

A special area should be reserved for the inspection and repair of films, filmstrips, recordings, slides and tapes which have been returned from circulation. The simple repair of audio-visual equipment may also be performed in this area. The area should be close to the entrance of the library and convenient to the circulation desk.

Most audio-visual equipment will be distributed from the library on short-term loans. The check-out of equipment should always be the responsibility of one person designated by the librarian. A student projectionist club could be formed to distribute and operate equipment under the librarian's supervision.

It is the responsibility of the head librarian to coordinate the services of the library and multimedia areas. Some examples of how

---

[1] American Library Association, *Standards for School Media Programs.* Chicago: American Library Association, 1969, pp. 41-43.

[2] Anna L. Hyer, "Setting Quantitative Standards," *Audio-Visual Instruction,* VI: 506-510, December 1961.

[3] National Audio-Visual Association, Inc., *The Audio-Visual Equipment Directory.* Fairfax, Virginia: NAVA, 1969.

ORGANIZATION OF MULTIMEDIA RESOURCES

the various areas of both the library and multimedia center can be coordinated within one administrative physical organization are shown in Appendix V. In all instances, the space provided for audio-visual material, equipment, repair, storage, and circulation must be planned in relation to the other functional areas of the library.

## CIRCULATION OF MULTIMEDIA MATERIAL

The circulation of multimedia material in the school library should follow the regular circulation routines for library books. Some specific recommendations for the various types of materials are provided below.

### Newspapers and Magazines

To circulate magazines and newspapers, temporary charge slips are recommended. (See Illusttration No. 12 for example of temporary mimeographed charge slip) These "periodical" items should be loaned for overnight use and allowed to circulate any time during the day. It is suggested that the temporary charge slips be inter-filed with the regular circulation. When the item is returned to the library, the discharge of the item consists of matching the temporary charge slip with the item, and discarding the temporary charge slip.

### Vertical File

Circulation of items in the vertical file should be done in the same manner as magazines and newspapers. Length of circulation period recommended is one week. Manila envelopes should be used to carry materials while in circulation.

### Other Materials

All materials, other than magazines, newspapers, and vertical file material, fall into this category. The use of these materials in the library should not require formal circulation. Only if items

```
┌─────────────────────────────────┐
│      Temporary Charge Slip      │
│                                 │
│   Jack and Jill      (call no.) │
│   April 1969                    │
│                                 │
│   ─────────────────────────     │
│   date due  │  borrower's name  │
│             │                   │
│             │                   │
│             │                   │
│             │                   │
│             │                   │
│             │                   │
│             │                   │
│             │                   │
└─────────────────────────────────┘
```

*Illustration No. 12. Temporary Charge Slip.*

are taken from the library should the librarian keep circulation records. The same techniques used with magazines, newspapers, and vertical file materials are to be utilized for these "other materials." At the time a person desires to take the item from the library, the librarian should make a temporary charge slip. The librarian must use his discretion in determining the kind of material in this category that may be circulated for home use. In many cases, the student can use the material at home, but some of the material, because of its cost, must be used only under supervision. Home use on an overnight basis, however, should be extended by the librarian in as many cases as possible.

# X

# EVALUATION OF THE ELEMENTARY SCHOOL LIBRARY

Evaluation of the library is an important phase of school library administration. Evaluation in the elementary school is relatively new, although the Southern Association of Colleges and Schools has used evaluative techniques for elementary school libraries in its accrediting procedures for some time. Other accrediting associations, however, have not developed evaluative techniques especially for the elementary school library. In most cases, where school officials have been desirous of evaluating the elementary school library, various standard high school evaluation forms have been used. The elementary school library is unique primarily because of the age and nature of the students enrolled in the school. Thus, an evaluation of the elementary school library must take into consideration the age group as well as the administration organization of the school. A common error on the part of the librarian has been that of assuming the "annual report" took care of the evaluation of the elementary library.

The purposes of an evaluation are different from those of an annual report. A report merely "reports" facts. The primary purpose of a library evaluation is to determine the effectiveness of the total library program in fulfilling its role in support of the philosophy and objectives of the school. All activities and services of the library and librarian must be directly or indirectly related to the achievement of the school's purposes and philosophy. Through evaluation, assumptions about library practices and services should be tested. Further, old goals and objectives for the library should be clarified and new or revised goals established.

The librarian should acquaint himself with the various evaluative techniques (i.e., surveys, subjective questionnaires, standardized tests, etc.) weighing the advantages and disadvantages of each. He should also study the typical standard evaluation forms for high school, junior high school, and elementary school libraries. With proper understanding of the purposes of an evaluation and a knowledge of the varieties of evaluation forms available on all levels, the librarian is ready to select an elementary school library evaluation form. Currently, a commercial type of an evaluation form is not available for the elementary school library. In the absence of a suitable commercial evaluation form, the librarian must develop a form of his own.

There are two types of evaluation forms which can be used: the comprehensive and the brief. The comprehensive evaluation should afford total coverage of the elementary school library and should be conducted every five years, or at the same time the school is evaluating other phases of its program. The brief evaluation should be very short, designed to measure only one or two aspects of the library's program and performed during the years between comprehensive evaluations. The librarian should be aware of the main advantages and disadvantages of each type of evaluation. The comprehensive evaluation consumes a great quantity of time in its development and its administration. The brief evaluation can be prepared and performed quickly by the librarian, and serves as a spot check between comprehensive evaluations.

Evaluations must be planned at least one year in advance so the librarian can keep and assemble the records necessary for a purposeful evaluation. As soon as the evaluation form is decided upon, the librarian should make a list of the types of library records necessary for the approaching evaluation. Records which are usually necessary for any type of evaluation are: circulation statistics, resources of the library collection, itemization of furnishing by area, number of square feet per named area, copies of the school and library philosophies, list of personnel and qualifications, and an itemized list of *all* services to students and faculty.

Careful study should be given to the preparation of the evaluative form. A sample of a comprehensive evaluation form follows in Appendix VI. In the preparation of the evaluation, the librarian should include several categories of information. Each category should be presented in such a way that all questions or statements can be answered objectively. The following categories should

# EVALUATION OF THE ELEMENTARY SCHOOL LIBRARY

be included in any elementary school library evaluation: school and library philosophy, book selection, physical facilities, personnel, finances, library resources, and services to students and faculty. Good sources which can aid one in the preparation of an evaluation form are *Evaluative Criteria*,[1] *Evaluative Criteria for Junior High Schools*,[2] and *Evaluating the Elementary School Library Program*.[3]

The evaluation should be conducted by a committee chaired by the librarian and composed of teachers and a member of the administrative staff. A committee of five members is recommended. Each member of the committee should conduct his evaluation individually; the chairman should then call the committee together for a compilation and summary. After the total evaluation is completed, scored, and a final evaluative rating is given, a summary should be prepared for the school acministrator. The summary should contain a copy of the instructions for administering the form, the committee's final evaluation, and recommendations for use of the results of the evaluation.

The librarian, faculty, and the school administrator can each utilize the evaluation results. The librarian should be first to use the evaluation findings to implement programs of improvements within the library organization; these improvements should follow the general categories of the evaluation form. For example, if the library did not have a written philosophy, the librarian, by following suggestions outlined in an earlier chapter of this book, can start steps immediately to develop a school library philosophy. Under the category of services to students and faculty, if the library was not open sufficient hours to allow adequate use of its resources, the librarian can work with the school administrator and teachers in trying to cooperatively arrange for better use of the library facilities.

---

[1] National Study of Secondary School Evaluation. *Evaluative Criteria.* Washington: National Study of Secondary School Evaluation, 1960.

[2] National Study of Secondary School Evaluation. *Evaluative Criteria for Junior High Schools.* Washington: National Study of Secondary School Evaluation, 1963.

[3] Southern Association of Colleges and Schools. *Evaluating the Elementary School Library Program.* Atlanta: The Association, n.d.

The school administrator is without doubt in the best position to make use of the evaluation results. The evaluation will inform the school administrator about his library, and armed with this information, he is now able to strengthen his requests for budgetary increases, personnel, and facilities. The school administrator's use of the information in the evaluation can be the basis for his endorsement of a system wide library program.

The faculty can learn through the findings of the evaluation, the extent of their use and their encouragement of the students' use of the library. Further, the faculty can determine the extent certain categories and types of materials are used. These are only a few of the suggested uses that may be made of the evaluation by the faculty. Departmental heads should exert leadership in using the evaluation findings to up-grade teaching and curriculum building.

The librarian should view the evaluation of the elementary library as a means of growth and development, and not as an end in itself. The elementary library as reflected evaluatively should parallel the evaluations of other phases of the school's program. Through evaluative techniques, library development within school systems and school districts can be measured and improvements of various facets of the library program in the different schools can be implemented. The librarian, therefore, is the real key to a successfully administered and organized library program.

# APPENDIX I.

## SCHOOL LIBRARY PHILOSOPHY

The Elementary School Library believes that its responsibility is to assist the school system in providing the best education for the youth of the school by supplying the students and teachers with the best possible information available in books, other resource materials and/or services of the library and librarian to enable them to achieve competencies and adjustment in personal, social, civic and vocational living.

## PURPOSES

The purposes of this library are to contribute to the attainment of the greatest achievement within the abilities of every child in self-realization, human relationships, economic efficiency and civic responsibility; to aid the teachers and administration in curriculum planning and development, and to provide for the proper storage, classification and cataloging of all materials.

## OBJECTIVES

1. Cooperate with the administration, faculty, and staff in the establishment of the library as an integral part of the total educational program.

2. Arouse in students an interest in books and other materials and broaden this interest through service in a pleasant atmosphere.

3. Provide continuous, progressive instruction in the use of the library, materials and services.

4. Make provision for attendance to and full use of the library materials and services by all students.

5. Provide for the continuous building of a reference collection to meet the needs of the curriculum and a broad collection of materials (books, periodicals, newspapers and audio visual aids) to meet the individual needs of the students.

6. Assist the administration in developing good public relations through pleasant and friendly contacts with students, teachers, staff and people of the community.

# APPENDIX II
## GRADE LEVEL FOR DEVELOPMENT OF LIBRARY SKILLS

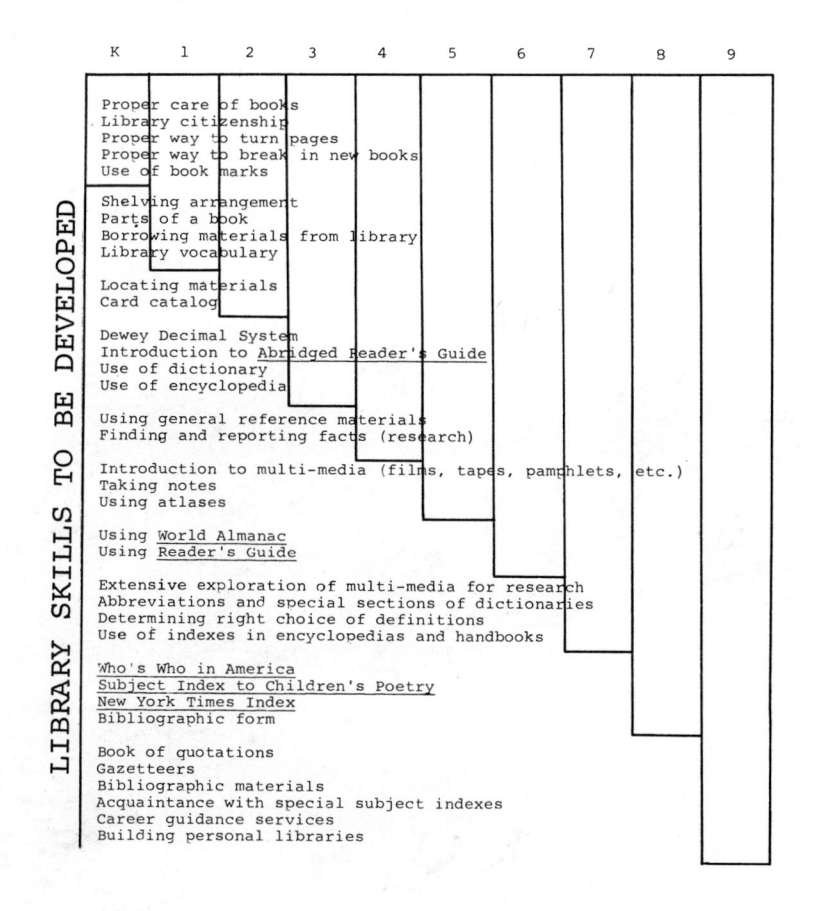

```
                     K    1    2    3    4    5    6    7    8    9
```

LIBRARY SKILLS TO BE DEVELOPED

Proper care of books
Library citizenship
Proper way to turn pages
Proper way to break in new books
Use of book marks

Shelving arrangement
Parts of a book
Borrowing materials from library
Library vocabulary

Locating materials
Card catalog

Dewey Decimal System
Introduction to Abridged Reader's Guide
Use of dictionary
Use of encyclopedia

Using general reference materials
Finding and reporting facts (research)

Introduction to multi-media (films, tapes, pamphlets, etc.)
Taking notes
Using atlases

Using World Almanac
Using Reader's Guide

Extensive exploration of multi-media for research
Abbreviations and special sections of dictionaries
Determining right choice of definitions
Use of indexes in encyclopedias and handbooks

Who's Who in America
Subject Index to Children's Poetry
New York Times Index
Bibliographic form

Book of quotations
Gazetteers
Bibliographic materials
Acquaintance with special subject indexes
Career guidance services
Building personal libraries

# APPENDIX III.

## UNIT PLAN FOR GRADE K

Proper Care of Books

Purposes:
    To develop an appreciation for books.
    To develop wholesome attitudes toward treatment of books.
    To develop self-discipline.

How achieved:
    After the first initial visit to the library, this unit may be presented.
    Things the children already know:
        The librarian's name.
        How to find the library in the school building.
        That the librarian is a teacher.
        That the librarian tells good stories to the children.
        That the librarian also reads good stories to the children.

    Presentation of the care of books and library discipline can be done effectively through the use of "Casper, the ghost" posters. Themes should center around these topics:
        Casper has clean hands.
        Casper keeps the tables neat.
        Casper turns pages carefully.
        Casper handles books with care.
        Casper does not crowd anyone.
        Casper takes books carefully from the shelves.
        Casper replaces books so that the title shows.
        Casper listens to stories without wiggling or talking.
        Casper lifts his chair out from the table.

# APPENDIX

Casper returns library materials on time.
Casper protects a book from rain, baby brother, and puppy.

After use of the posters, a simple game can be played, "What else does Casper do?"

# APPENDIX IV.

## FILING EXAMPLES [1,2]

In filing, disregard punctuation marks and file in a straight alphabet word by word.

Deep down under

Defoe, Daniel

DeJong, Dola — Proper names with a prefix are arranged as one word.

Delacroix, Eugene

De Leeuw, Adele

Del Rey, Lester

DEMOCRACY

FBI see U.S. Federal Bureau of Investigation — Initials are arranged at the beginning of each letter.

The FDR story

The fish and the ring

Fish, Helen Dean

Fisher, Aileen

FISHING—FLIES see FLIES, ARTIFICIAL
— Hyphened words are filed as separate words when the parts are complete words.

FIVE-DAY WORK WEEK see HOURS OF LABOR

FOLK LORE see FOLKLORE

FOLK TALES see FOLKLORE

[1] For additional information or rules see *ALA Rules for Filing Catalog Cards,* 2d ed. abridged, Chicago: American Library Association, 1968.
[2] These examples are for a dictionary catalog; for a divided card catalog merely pull out the subject entries (in capital letters) and arrange separately.

# APPENDIX

FOLKLORE — Choose one spelling and file all entries under that spelling with a "see" reference from other spellings.

4-H CLUBS — Numerals are arranged as spelled out in the languages of the entry.

FOURTH OF JULY

FRANCE—HISTORY

FRANCE — HISTORY — To 1328 — Periods of history are arranged chronologically then subdivisions of "History" are arranged alphabetically.

FRANCE—HISTORY—
BOURBORS, 1589-1789.

FRANCE—HISTORY—
REVOLUTION, 1789-1799

FRANCE—HISTORY—
1914-1940.

FRANCE—HISTORY—
GERMAN OCCUPATION, 1940-1945.

FRANCE—HISTORY—1958

FRANCE—HISTORY—
BIBLIOGRAPHY

FRANCE—HISTORY—
OUTLINE, SYLLABI, ETC.

Franklin, Benjamin
Autobiography of Benjamin Franklin — Works by an author are arranged first alphabetical by title then works about him alphabetical by main entry.

Franklin, Benjamin
Poor Richard's Almanack

FRANKLIN, BENJAMIN
Daugherty, Jeaneet
That lively man, Ben Franklin

Macauley, Edward

McCall's guide to teen-age beauty and glamour — Mc and Mac are arranged together under Mac.

McCloskey, Robert
Blueberries for Sal — Main entries and secondary entries are interfiled by title.

McCloskey, Robert, Illus.
Robertson, Keith
Henry Reed, Inc.

McCloskey, Robert
Homer Price

McCloskey, Robert
Make way for ducklings

83

McGrady, Mike

MACHINE TOOLS

MACHINERY see also Hydraulic Machinery. See also cards are filed before other entries of the same word.

MACHINERY

MACHINERY—DESIGN

MACHINERY IN INDUSTRY

Mr. Revere and I — Abbreviations are arranged as spelled in full.

Mrs. Wiggs of the cabbage patch — Mrs. is an exception.

# APPENDIX V. FLOOR PLANS

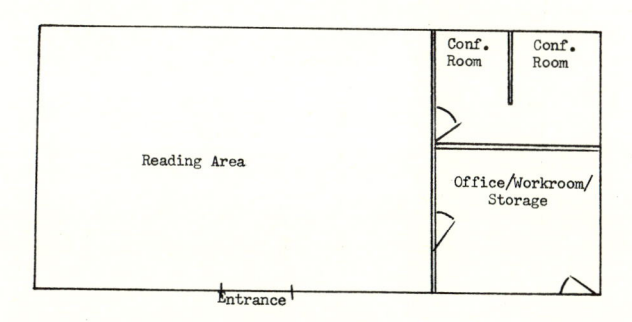

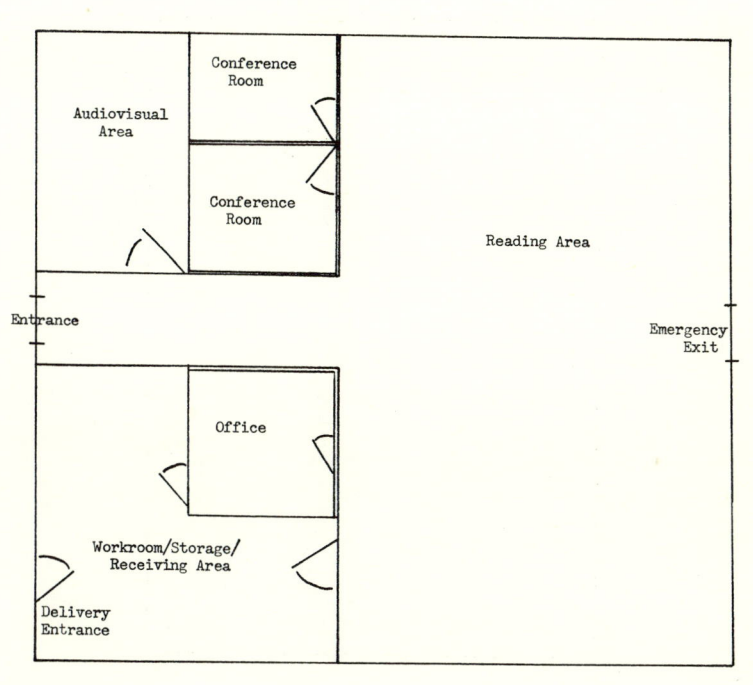

Audiovisual Area

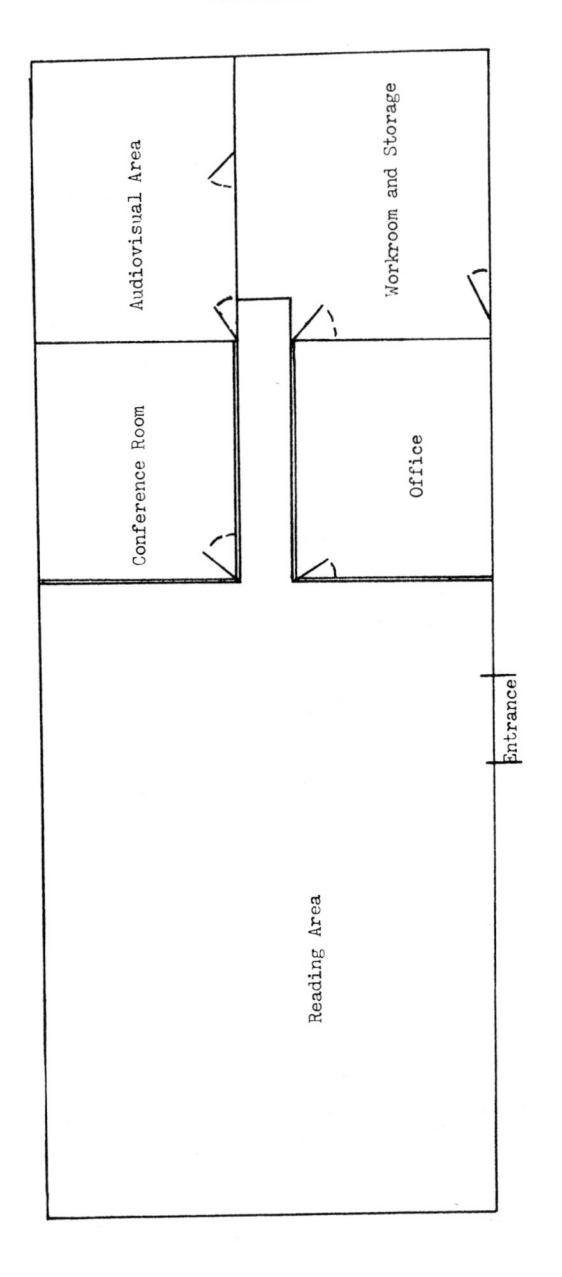

Workroom and Storage

Conference Room

Office

Entrance

Reading Area

APPENDIX

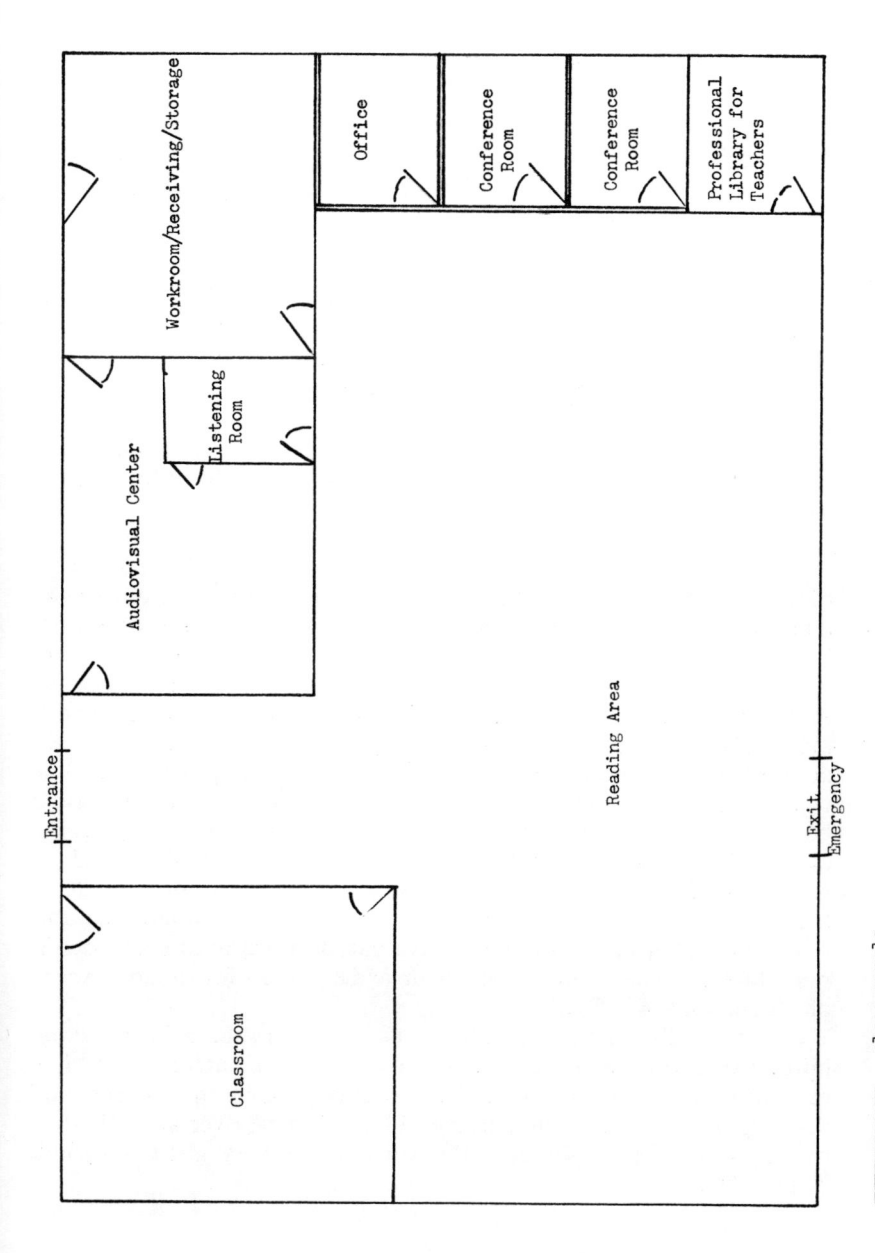

― glass panels.

# APPENDIX VI.

## ELEMENTARY SCHOOL LIBRARY EVALUATION FORM

Directions:

This evaluation attempts to assist the library administrator in determining the effectiveness of the library's total program as an integral unit of the elementary school. The evaluation should be performed by a committee appointed by the library administrator in cooperation with the school administrator; each committee member should self-administer the evaluation. The evaluation should result in an accurate assessment of the objectives of the library in relation to the total school program.

The evaluative form contains two parts. Part I, "Evaluation of the Elementary School Library", contains statements characteristic of an excellent library and consistent with recommendations of the American Library Association, the American Association of School Librarians, and the National Education Association. The form provides three columns which the evaluation committee should complete. In Column I, the committee should record the State Department of Education's recommendations; Column II, the school's actual situation for each item; Column III, the evaluative score. The evaluative score which the committee records in Column III, should be determined as follows: If the school library meets the requirements of the statement fully, a "1" equivalent to "yes" should be recorded; if the school library does not meet the requirements of the statement a "0" equivalent to "no" should be recorded. Sections A through G of Part I should be evaluated and a total score determined for each section. Section H provides blanks for the total score of all sections A - G.

Part II, "Summary of Evaluation", provides spaces for the committee to record each sectional score and an evaluative rating. The evaluative rating is determined by adding total points scored and dividing by the total possible points. The following over-all evaluative ratings should be observed: 100-excellent; 90-very good; 80-good; 70-fair; 60-poor.

# APPENDIX

# Part I. Evaluation Of The Elementary School Library[1]

|  | STATE RECOM- MENDA- TIONS | ACTUAL SITUA- TIONS | EVALU- ATIVE SCORE |
|---|---|---|---|

### A. School Philosophy

1. The school has a written philosophy of education. ___ ___ ___

2. The philosophy contains specific purposes and objectives. ___ ___ ___

3. The school philosophy has been re-evaluated within the past 5 years. ___ ___ ___

4. The school philosophy was prepared by the school board with the cooperation of the faculty and the school administration. ___ ___ ___

Total points for "A" — (4 possible) ___

### B. School Library Philosophy

1. The school library has a written philosophy. ___ ___ ___

2. Specific purposes and objectives are written. ___ ___ ___

3. The library philosophy has been re-evaluated within the past 5 years. ___ ___ ___

4. The library philosophy was prepared by a committee chaired by the librarian and made up of faculty and the school administrator. ___ ___ ___

Total points for "B" — (4 possible) ___

[1] It is recommended that this form be used in the evaluation of a single library.

|  | STATE RECOM- MENDA- TIONS | ACTUAL SITUA- TIONS | EVALU- ATIVE SCORE |
|---|---|---|---|

*C. Physical Facilities*

1. The reading area is large enough to seat 50 students or 15 percent of the school's enrollment.

2. Tables and chairs are provided in various sizes to accommodate C(1) above.

3. A minimum of 30 percent of the study spaces are individualized.

4. Shelving can accommodate a book collection of 10,000 books.

5. The entrance area has a minimum of 800 sq. ft. to accommodate displays, exhibits, bulletin boards, and circulation and distribution of materials.

6. A special storytelling area is provided in the library.

7. A magazine storage space of 250 sq. ft. is available.

8. A minimum of 3 conference rooms of 150 sq. ft. are provided in the library.

9. An area of 600 sq. ft. is provided in the form of a professional reading room for faculty.

10. An audiovisual storage and processing area is part of the library.

11. A small group viewing and listening room is provided in the library.

APPENDIX

|  | STATE RECOMMENDATIONS | ACTUAL SITUATIONS | EVALUATIVE SCORE |
|---|---|---|---|

12. A workroom with a minimum of 300 sq. ft. is provided for the librarian. ⎯⎯ ⎯⎯ ⎯⎯

13. Office space is provided for the professional staff. ⎯⎯ ⎯⎯ ⎯⎯

14. A maintenance and repair service area contains at least 120 sq. ft. ⎯⎯ ⎯⎯ ⎯⎯

15. Stack area of 400 sq. ft. is available for overflow books and audiovisual materials. ⎯⎯ ⎯⎯ ⎯⎯

Total points for "C" — (15 possible) ⎯⎯

D. *Personnel*

1. There is a properly certified librarian for each 250 students. ⎯⎯ ⎯⎯ ⎯⎯

2. There are two non-professional persons employed full time for each librarian. ⎯⎯ ⎯⎯ ⎯⎯

3. A professional audiovisual specialist is part of the library staff. ⎯⎯ ⎯⎯ ⎯⎯

4. Student assistants, if used, are paid on the minimum wage scale. ⎯⎯ ⎯⎯ ⎯⎯

Total points for "D" — (4 possible) ⎯⎯

E. *Finances*

1. Annual budget appropriations for library resources are equal to 6 percent of the national average pupil operational cost per student. ⎯⎯ ⎯⎯ ⎯⎯

**FORSYTH LIBRARY**
**FORT HAYS KANSAS STATE COLLEGE**

|  | STATE RECOMMENDATIONS | ACTUAL SITUATIONS | EVALUATIVE SCORE |
|---|---|---|---|

2. The library budget allows 3 percent of the above amount per pupil expenditure for printed materials and 3 percent for non-print materials.   ____ ____ ____

3. The salary scale of the library staff is on the same basis as other professional school employees.   ____ ____ ____

Total points for "E" — (3 possible)   ____

F. *Library Resources*

1. The library general book collection contains 10,000 volumes.   ____ ____ ____

2. A collection of appropriate pamphlets, clippings, documents, etc. is available to students and staff.   ____ ____ ____

3. The library has 500 filmstrips available for use.   ____ ____ ____

4. The library has 500 single concept films.   ____ ____ ____

5. The library subscribes to 3 newspapers.   ____ ____ ____

6. The library subscribes to 50 periodicals.   ____ ____ ____

7. A collection of 200 professional books is available for faculty use.   ____ ____ ____

8. The library has 40 professional journals, plus *Education Index,* accessible to the faculty.   ____ ____ ____

# APPENDIX

|  | STATE RECOMMENDATIONS | ACTUAL SITUATIONS | EVALUATIVE SCORE |
|---|---|---|---|
| 9. Tape and disc recordings number 1,000. | | | |
| 10. The library has 2,000 transparencies. | | | |
| 11. One thousand pieces of graphic materials are available. | | | |
| 12. The slide collection contains 2,000 slides. | | | |
| 13. There are two globes in the library. | | | |
| 14. There is one map in the library for each region and area studied in the curriculum. | | | |
| 15. All library materials are cataloged. | | | |
| 16. Materials are purchased regularly. | | | |
| 17. All materials are shelved and stored in areas easily accessible to students and faculty. | | | |
| 18. Materials are repaired systematically. | | | |
| 19. Materials are weeded continuously. | | | |
| 20. Periodical back files are available on film. | | | |
| 21. The library has a written selection policy for all print and non-print materials. | | | |
| 22. Selections are made on staff recommendations. | | | |
| 23. Selections are also made on pupil recommendations. | | | |

|  | STATE RECOM- MENDA- TIONS | ACTUAL SITUA- TIONS | EVALU- ATIVE SCORE |
|---|---|---|---|
| 24. Interlibrary lending is practiced. | ___ | ___ | ___ |
| 25. Professional aids are used in book selection. | ___ | ___ | ___ |
| 26. The library maintains proper subject balance in the materials collection. | ___ | ___ | ___ |
| 27. The book collection represents all grade levels and all areas of interest. | ___ | ___ | ___ |
| 28. The library contains a sufficient quantity of reference books. | ___ | ___ | ___ |
| 29. At least one set of encyclopedias carries a copyright of this year. | ___ | ___ | ___ |
| 30. All library materials are circulated freely. | ___ | ___ | ___ |
| Total points for "F" — (30 possible) |  |  | ___ |

G. *Services to Pupils and Faculty*

1. Pupils are taught library skills through formal instruction. ___ ___ ___

2. Regular use of library facilities is encouraged for classroom purposes. ___ ___ ___

3. Students are encouraged to do free reading. ___ ___ ___

4. Students have access to the library before, during, and after school. ___ ___ ___

5. Students are taught research methods by the librarian. ___ ___ ___

APPENDIX

|  | STATE RECOM- MENDA- TIONS | ACTUAL SITUA- TIONS | EVALU- ATIVE SCORE |
|---|---|---|---|

6. Reference service is available throughout the school day. _____ _____ _____

7. Book lists and bibliographies are regularly prepared for teachers. _____ _____ _____

8. Teachers and librarian plan cooperatively for effective library use. _____ _____ _____

9. Pupils are able to visit the library any time a need arises. _____ _____ _____

10. Librarian provides services to teachers during a workshop prior to the opening of school. _____ _____ _____

11. Librarian offers consultant services to teachers. _____ _____ _____

12. Librarian keeps teachers informed of new materials. _____ _____ _____

13. Librarian assists teachers in development of units instruction involving library use. _____ _____ _____

14. Student organizations are encouraged to use the library facilities. _____ _____ _____

15. Story hours are provided for all grades. _____ _____ _____

16. Sessions are held between the librarian and faculty to discuss reading problems of students. _____ _____ _____

17. Librarian makes frequent informal reports to the administrator. _____ _____ _____

|  | STATE RECOM- MENDA- TIONS | ACTUAL SITUA- TIONS | EVALU- ATIVE SCORE |
|---|---|---|---|
| 18. Librarian seeks cooperation of teachers in any disciplinary problem in the library. | ___ | ___ | ___ |
| 19. Librarian holds special in-service training for new teachers. | ___ | ___ | ___ |
| 20. Attractive bulletin boards are prepared with current school activities. | ___ | ___ | ___ |
| 21. Exhibits of realia are arranged. | ___ | ___ | ___ |
| 22. A resource file is maintained for the teachers. | ___ | ___ | ___ |
| 23. Librarian seeks book recommendations from teachers and children. | ___ | ___ | ___ |
| 24. Book discussions are conducted. | ___ | ___ | ___ |
| 25. Book talks are presented in cooperation with the teachers. | ___ | ___ | ___ |
| 26. A library student assistant program is planned cooperatively with the teachers. | ___ | ___ | ___ |
| 27. A library information handbook is provided for pupils, parents, and teachers. | ___ | ___ | ___ |
| 28. The librarian participates actively in local, state, and national professional organizations of both education and library professions. | ___ | ___ | ___ |
| 29. The librarian serves on teaching teams. | ___ | ___ | ___ |
| Total points for "G" — (29 possible) |  |  | ___ |

APPENDIX

|  | STATE RECOM- MENDA- TIONS | ACTUAL SITUA- TIONS | EVALU- ATIVE SCORE |

*H. Total Score*

(89 possible points)    actual score

*I. Committee Recommendations*

_____
(Chairman)                    (Date)
_____
_____
_____
_____

# PART II. SUMMARY OF EVALUATION.

_____
Name of school

_____
Name of library

_____
Pupil/teacher ratio

A.  SCHOOL PHILOSOPHY

    Comments:

    Score_____

    Evaluative rating_____

B.  THE SCHOOL LIBRARY PHILOSOPHY

    Comments:

    Score_____

    Evaluative rating_____

C.  PHYSICAL FACILITIES

    Comments:

    Score_____

    Evaluative rating_____

APPENDIX 99

D. PERSONNEL

    Comments:

    Score_____

    Evaluative rating_____

E. FINANCES

    Comments:

    Score_____

    Evaluative rating_____

F. LIBRARY RESOURCES

    Comments:

    Score_____

    Evaluative rating_____

G. SERVICES TO PUPILS AND FACULTY

    Comments:

    Score_____

    Evaluative rating_____

H.  OVER-ALL EVALUATIVE SCORE = $\dfrac{89}{X}$ = _____

      Possible score: __89__

      Actual score: __X__


I.  COMMITTEE RECOMMENDATIONS




_____
(Chairman)                    (Date)

_____

_____

_____

_____

# SELECTED BIBLIOGRAPHY

## I. HISTORY AND PHILOSOPHY

Cecil, Henry L. *School Library Service in the United States*. New York: H. W. Wilson, 1940.

Educational Policies Commission. *The Purposes of Education in American Democracy*. Washington: National Education Association, 1938.

Henry, Nelson B. ed. *The Forty-Second Yearbook of the National Society for the Study of Education, Part II, The Library in General Education*. Chicago: University of Chicago Press, 1943.

U.S. Department of Health, Education and Welfare, Office of Education. *Survey of School Library Standards*. Washington: U.S. Government Printing Office, 1964.

U.S. Office of Education. *Bienniel Survey of Education in the U.S. 1941-42*. Washington: Government Printing Office, 1945.

## II. ADMINISTRATION AND ORGANIZATION

*A. L. A. Glossary of Library Terms*. Chicago: American Library Association, 1943.

Akers, Susan Grey, *Simple Library Cataloging*. Metuchen, N. J.: Scarecrow Press, 1969.

American Association of School Librarians. *Standards for School Library Programs*. Chicago: American Library Association, 1960.

American Library Association. *ALA Rules for Filing Catalog Cards*. 2d ed. abridged. Chicago: American Library Association, 1968.

American Library Association. *Standards for School Media Programs*. Chicago: American Library Association, 1969.

*The Bowker Annual Library and Book Trade Information*. New York: R. R. Bowker Company.

Cutter, Charles A. *Alphabetic Order Table Altered and Fitted with Three Figures,* by Kate E. Sanborn. Chicopee Falls, Massachusetts: H. R. Huntting Company.

Dewey, Melvil. *Dewey Decimal Classification and Relative Index.* 9th abridged ed. Lake Placid, N.Y.: Forest Press. 1965.

Gould, Geraldine N. and Ithmer C. Wolfe. *How to Organize and Maintain the Library Picture Pamphlet File.* Dobbs Ferry, N. Y.: Oceana Publications, Inc., 1968.

Hopkinson, Shirley L. *The Descriptive Cataloging of Library Materials.* 3d ed. rev. and enl. San Jose, Calif.: Claremont House, 1968.

Lowrie, Jean Elizabeth. *Elementary School Libraries.* New York: Scarecrow Press, Inc., 1961.

McGinniss, Dorothy A., ed. *Libraries and Youth: Cooperation to Give Services to Children and Young People.* Syracuse: School of Library Science, 1968.

Mahar, Mary Helen, ed. *The School Library as a Materials Center.* Washington: U. S. Office of Education, 1963. (OE-15042 Circular No. 708).

National Education Association, Department of Audiovisual Instruction. *Standards for Cataloging, Coding and Scheduling Educational Media.* Washington, D. C.: National Education Association, 1968.

Piercy, Esther J. *Commonsense Cataloging; A Manual for the Organization of Books and Other Materials in School and Small Public Libraries.* New York: H. W. Wilson Company 1965.

Saunders, Helen E. *The Modern School Library; Its Administration as a Materials Center.* Metuchen, N. J.: Scarecrow Press, 1968.

Sears, Minnie E. *Sears List of Subject Headings.* Edited by Barbara Marietta Westby. 9th ed. New York: H. W. Wilson Company, 1965.

Westhuis, Judith Loveys and Julia M. DeYoung. *Cataloging Manual for Nonbook Materials in Learning Centers and School Libraries.* Rev. ed. Ann Arbor, Michigan: Michigan Association of School Librarians, 1967.

## III. SELECTION OF BOOKS

*Basic Book Collection for Elementary Grades.* 7th ed. Chicago: American Library Association, 1960.

# SELECTED BIBLIOGRAPHY

*Basic Book Collection for Junior High Schools.* 3d ed. Chicago: American Library Association, 1960.

*Best Books for Children.* New York: R. R. Bowker. (Annual)

*Books in Print; an Author-Title-Series Index to the Publishers' Trade List Annual.* 3 volumes. New York: R. R. Bowker Company. (Annual)

*Bulletin of the Center for Children's Books.* Chicago: University of Chicago Press. (monthly September-July)

*Children's Catalog.* Edited by Rachel Shor and Estelle A. Fidell. 11th ed. New York: H. W. Wilson Company, 1966. (Supplements)

Eakin, Mary K. *Good Books for Children; a Selection of Outstanding Children's Books Published, 1950-1965.* 3d ed. Chicago: University of Chicago Press, 1966.

Eakin, Mary K. and Eleanor Merritt. *Subject Guide to Books for Primary Grades.* Chicago: American Library Association, 1961.

*Elementary English; a Magazine of the Language Arts.* Champaign, Ill.: National Council of Teachers of English. (Monthly October-May)

*The Elementary School Library Collection.* General editor, Mary V. Gaver. 3d ed. Newark, N. J.: Bro Dart Foundation, 1967.

*Guide to Children's Magazines, Newspapers, and Reference Books.* Association for Childhood Education International.

*Junior High School Library Catalog.* Edited by Rachel Shor and Estelle A. Fidell. 1st ed. New York: H. W. Wilson Company, 1965. (Supplements)

Larrick, Nancy. *A Parent's Guide to Children's Reading.* Rev. ed. Garden City, N. Y.: Doubleday and Company, 1964.

Larrick, Nancy. *A Teacher's Guide to Children's Books.* Columbus, Ohio: Charles E. Merrill Books, Inc., 1960.

*Booklist and Subscription Books Bulletin.* Chicago: American Library Association. (Twice a month September through July, once in August)

*The Horn Book Magazine.* Boston: Horn Book, Inc. (Bimonthly)

*Library Journal.* New York: R. R. Bowker. (Twice a month September through June, monthly in July and August)

*School Library Journal.* New York: R. R. Bowker. (Monthly September through June. Issued separately or as part of *Library Journal* on the fifteenth of each month)

*Textbooks in Print.* New York: R. R. Bowker Company. (Annual)

*Wilson Library Bulletin.* New York: H. W. Wilson Company. (Monthly September-June)

## IV. MULTIMEDIA

*Audio-Visual Instruction.* Washington, D. C.: Department of Audio-Visual Instruction, National Education Association. (Monthly except July-September)

*A-V Communication Review.* Washington, D. C.: Department of Audio-Visual Instruction, National Education Association. (Quarterly)

*Children's Record Catalog.* New York: Harrison Record Catalogs. (Annually)

*Education Age Magazine.* Minnesota Mining and Manufacturing Company. (5 times a year)

*Educational Film Guide.* New York: H. W. Wilson. (Annually)

*Educational Media Index:* A Project of the Educational Media Council. New York: McGraw Hill, 1964. 14 volumes.

*Educators Guide to Free Films.* Randolph, Wis.: Educators Progress Service. (Annually)

*Educators Guide to Free Guidance Materials.* Randolph, Wis.: Educators Progress Service (Annual)

*Educators Guide to Free Filmstrips.* Randolph, Wis.: Educators Progress Service. (Annually)

*Educators Guide to Media and Methods.* New York: Media and Methods Institute, Inc. (Monthly)

# SELECTED BIBLIOGRAPHY

*Educators Guide to Free Science Materials.* Randolph, Wis.: Educators Progress Service. (Annually)

*Educators Guide to Free Social Studies Materials.* Randolph, Wis.: Educators Progress Service. (Annually)

*Educators Guide to Free Tapes, Scripts and Transcriptions.* Randolph Wis.: Educators Progress Service. (Annual) (Annotated list of free tapes, scripts and transcriptions)

*Educators Index of Free Materials.* Card File. Randolph, Wis.: Educators Progress Service. (Annually)

*Grade Teacher.* Darien, Conn.: Teachers Publishing Corporation. (Monthly September-May)

*Index to 16mm Educational Films.* New York: McGraw Hill, 1967.

*Index of 35mm Educational Filmstrips.* New York: McGraw Hill, 1968.

*Magazines for Libraries.* New York: Bowker, 1968.

*National Tape Recording Catalog.* Washington, D. C.: Department of Audio-Visual Instruction, National Education Association and other, 1954.

*PTA Magazine.* Chicago: National Congress of Parents and Teachers. (Monthly September-June)

*Recordings for Children, a selected list.* 2d ed. New York: Library Association, 1964.

*U. S. Government Films for Public Educational Use.* Washington, D. C.: U. S. Government Printing Office.

*Vertical File Index; A Subject and Title Index to Selected Pamphlet Material.* Bronx, N. Y.: H. W. Wilson. (Monthly)

# INDEX

Accession book, 38
Accession number, 35, 38, 65
Accrediting associations, 21-22
Acquisitions, 32-36
    Methods of, 31-32
    Multimedia, 61-63
    Program, 32
Added entries, 36, 43-44
    Example, 40-41
Administration of school libraries, 25-28
    Agreements, 26
    By Board of Education, 25
    By public library, 26
    Forms of control, 25-26
    Types, 25
Aims, school library, 11
    Definition, 11
    Examples, 11
American Association of School Librarians, 5, 23
American Library Association, 3, 5, 6, 7, 10, 11, 21, 22, 28, 60
Americans, 1
Annual report, 73
Appropriations, 4
Architect, 52
Architecture and building, see Facilities, physical
Audio-visual, see Multimedia
Audio-visual clubs, 49
**Audio-Visual Equipment Directory,** 70
**Audio-Visual Instruction,** 62
Audio-visual room, 52-53, 56-57, 59-60
**Basic Book Collection for Junior High Schools,** 31
Bibliographies, 49, 51
Bibliotherapy, 14
Binding, 45
Board of Education, 25-27, 30

Book cards, 42-43, 48
    Example, 42
Book collection, 1, 29
    Development, 4
Book examination, 36-37
Book fair, 49
Book jackets, 14, 43
Book pocket, 42-43, 48
    Example, 42
Book repair, 45
Book requests, 29-30
    Faculty requests, 29
    Form, 30
    Student requests, 29
Book selection, 24
    Award lists, 31
    Committee, 29-30, 62
    Committee responsibility, 29
    Criteria (fiction), 31
    Criteria (non-fiction), 31
    Librarian's responsibility, 29-31
    Policies, 30-31
    School administrator, 29
    Series, 31
Book selection aids, 30-31
Book selection sources, 31-32
Book stores, 33
Book talks, 49
Book withdrawals, 42, 45
    Loss, 42
    Missing, 44-45
**Books In Print,** 33
**Bowker Annual,** 43
Browsing, 49
Budget, 32, 50
**Bulletin of the Center for Children's Books,** 31
Call number, 36-37, 42, 48, 63, 65
Card catalog, 43-44, 63, 69
    Labels, 43-44
Cards, guide, 43
Carnegie Corporation, 5

Catalog cards, 63, 65
    Preparation, 38-43
    Set (example), 40-41
Cataloging, 35-43
    Books: steps to follow, 36-43
    Multimedia, 63, 65, 69
Cataloging work slip, 36
Censorship, 31
Certain, C. C., 4
"Certain Report", 3-4
Charts, 61
**Children's Catalog,** 31, 33
Children's reading, 13-14
Circulation, 46-49
    Discharge, 48
    Fines, 48
    Equipment, 47-48
    Loan period, 48
    Multimedia resources, 71-72
    Periodicals, 71
    Records, 48
    Systems,
        automatic, 47
        manual, 47
    Types of,
        non-permissive, 46-47
        permissive, 46-47
    Vertical file, 71
Civil War, 2
Classification of books, 37-38
Clerical assistant, 22-23
    Duties, 22-23
    Number of, 22
    Qualifications, 22
    Salary, 23
Clinton, Gov. DeWitt, 1-2
Clippings, 61
College courses, 7
Community, 10, 46
Conference room, 53, 56-57, 58-59
County-wide school library administration, 27-28
    Advantages, 27-28
    Director of, 27-28

Director, duties, 27
Curriculum committee, 51
Curriculum planning, 51
**Cutter** number, 37-38
Date due, 48, 63
Date due slip, 42
    Example, 42
Desk Attendant, 48
**Dewey Decimal Classification and Relative Index,** 36-37
Dutch, 1
Educational Facilities Laboratories, 60
**Educational Media Index,** 62
Educational Policies Commission, 10
Elementary and Secondary Education Act, 7
    Effects of, 7-8
    Provisions of, 7
**Elementary English,** 31
Elementary school libraries
    Centralized, 3-5
    Decline, 2
    Financial stimulation, 5
    History, 1-8
    Number, 2, 4
    Recommendations, 5-6
    Twentieth century, 3-5
**Elementary School Library Collection,** 31, 33, 36
Elementary school system, 4
English, 1
Equipment, see Facilities, physical
Europe, 1
**Evaluating the Elementary School Library Program,** 47
Evaluation, 73-76
    Brief, 74-75
    Categories, 74
    Comprehensive, 74
    Form, 74
    Multimedia, 62
    Records, 74

# INDEX

Techniques, 74
  Use, 75-76
Evaluation committee, 75
**Evaluative Criteria,** 75
**Evaluative Criteria for Junior High Schools,** 75
Exhibits, 14, 62
Exploratory units, 2
Facilities, physical, 5, 52-60
  Areas, 53-60
  Floor plan, 53-54
  Planning, 52
  Remodeled, 52, 60
  Requirements, 52-53
Federal funds, 5-8
Filing of catalog cards, 43-44
  Revising, 44
Film, 59, 61, 69, 70
  Symbol, 65
  Repair, 70
Filmstrip,
  Preview, 62
  Symbol, 65
  Repair, 70
Fines, 48
**Fourth Yearbook of the NEA, Department of Elementary School Principals,** 3
France, 1
French, 1
Functions, school library, 12-20
  Four areas, 11-12
Furnishings, see Furniture
Furniture, 47-48, 53-60, 74
  Chart, 55-56
Game, 69
  Symbol, 65
Globe, 61, 69
  Symbol, 65
**Grade Teacher,** 31
Graphics, 69
  Storage, 60
  Symbol, 65
Graphs, 61

Group guidance, 14-15
  Examples, 15
Group instruction, 18
**Guide to Free Tapes, Transcriptions, and Recordings,** 62
Hobbies, 14
**Horn Book,** 31
Illinois, 4
Independent research, 19-20
  Definition, 20
Individual guidance, 15-16
  Examples, 15-16
Individual instruction, 18
  Example, 18-19
"Instituteur", 1
Instruction, library use, 16-19
  Cooperative program, 19
  Formal, 16, 18
  Informal, 16, 18-19
Instructional materials specialist, 7
Instructional program, 46
Inter-library loans, 50
Inventory, 44-45
Invoices, payment of, 35
Iowa, 4
Jobber catalogs, 31
Jobbers, advantages and disadvantages, 33
Julius Rosenwald Fund, 5
**Junior High School Library Catalog,** 31, 33, 36
Kits, 69
  Symbol, 65
Labeling, 43, 63
Language laboratory, 60
Learning center, 60
Legislation, 2
Librarian, 61-62, 70
  Characteristics, 21-22
  Duties, 22
  In community, 51
  Office, 53, 57-58
  Professional education, 21
  Qualifications, 21

Responsibilities, 9, 11-16, 46-50, 52, 74-76
Librarians, demand, 7
Librarians, employment, 4
Libraries, 1
Library, 2
　Club, 49
　Handbook, 50
　Visits, 12
Library development, 2, 4, 26
　Guidelines, 4-6
　Reasons for slowness, 4
　Recommendations (ALA), 5
Library instruction, 12
　Schedule (example), 17
**Library Journal,** 31, 33
Library ownership stamp, 35
Library paper, 49
Library request form (example), 30
Library personnel, 4
Magazines, see Periodicals
Main entry card, 38, 42-44, 63, 67
　Example, 39
Maps, 61, 69
　Storage, 60
　Symbol, 65
Massachusetts, 4
Media specialist, 21
Models, 61, 69
　Symbol, 65
Multimedia Resources, 61-72
　Area physical organization, 69-71
　Acquisitions, 61-63
　Cataloging and Processing, 61, 63, 65, 69
　Circulation, 71-72
　Definition, 61
　Evaluation, 62
　Leased, 63
　Main entry cards (examples), 66-68
　Processing, 61
　Selection, 61-62

Multimedia circulation, 48
Multiple order form, 34
　Example, 34
　Uses of, 33, 35
Multi-system library administration, 27
　Advantages, 27
　Conditions for, 27-28
　Types of administrative organizations, 27
National Council of Teachers of English, 5
National Defense Education Act, 5-6, 61
National Education Association, 3, 5
　Department of Audio-Visual Instruction, 62
National Education Week, 11
National Library Week, 11
National Tape Repository, 62
Negro, 5
New Nederland, 1
New York, 1, 2, 4
Newspapers, see Periodicals
Objectives, school library, 9-11, 73, 74
　American Library Association, 10-11
Occupational guidance leaflets, 61
Open house, 51
Order slip, 44
Ordering, frequency, 32
Ordering books
　Choosing vendor, 33
　Order form, 33, 35
　Placing order, 33, 35
　School district regulations, 35
Orders outstanding, 33, 35
Packing slip, 35
Pamphlets, 61, 69
Parents, 49, 51
Periodical holdings card, 63
　Example, 64
Periodicals, 63-64, 69

# INDEX

Circulation, 71
　Storage rooms, 53, 56-57
Personnel, library, 21-24
Philosophy, 9-11
　Library, 9, 72-75
　Revision, 11
　School, 47
Philosophy, educational, 2
Philosophy, formulation of, 9
　Committee, 9-11
　Committee duties, 9
Pictures, 61, 69
Pre-processed
　Books, 43
　Cards, 43
Preview sheets, 62
Processing books, 36-43
Processing multimedia, 61, 63, 65, 69
Professional materials, 50
Professional reading room, 53, 56-57, 59
Programmed texts, 69
　Symbol, 65
Projectionist Club, 70
Projectors
　Filmstrip, 59
　Movie, 59
Public education, 1
Public libraries, cooperation, 3
Public library, 49
Public services, 46-51
Publisher, ordering from, 33
Publishers' catalogs, 31
Publishers' displays, 31
Purposes
　Library, 10, 74
　School, 10
Radio
　Storage, 60
**Rapports des agents du ministre de l'intérieur dan des départments,** 1
**Reader's Guide to Periodical Literature,** 69
Reader's record, 48

Reading
　Desire, 13
　Factors affecting, 12
　For pleasure, 12-13
　Free reading, 12
　Pacers, 61
　Specialist, 49
Reading guidance, 13-16
　Librarian's role, 12-13
　Techniques for, 14
　Types, 14
Reading room, 53, 56-58, 69
　Area, 53
　Furniture, 53, 56-58
Realia, 61
Receiving and sorting room, 53, 56-57, 59
Record player, 58
Recordings, 62, 69-70
　Repair, 70
　Shelving, 58-59
　Symbol, 65
Recordings, tape, 69-70
　Symbol, 65
Reference
　Books, 20, 29
　　Circulation, 47
Request forms, 63
Research
　For administrator, 51
　Methods, 49
Reserve books, 48
Restrooms, 53, 56-57
Room libraries, 3
　Teacher reactions, 3
School administrator, 4, 9, 11, 23, 46-47, 49, 50-52, 69, 75-76
　Responsibility, 25-26
School budget, 4
School district, 2, 47
School district libraries, 2
School district library development, 9
School district library supervisor, 26

Duties, 26
Qualifications, 26
School equipment, 2
School libraries
    Elementary schools, 1
    History, 1-8
    New York, 2
**School Libraries for Today and Tomorrow**, 5
School library "Bill of Rights", 30
School library development, 7
School library supervisor, 9
School system, 6
Searching, 32-33
**Sear's List of Subject Headings**, 36, 38, 44
Secretarial assistant, 22-23
    Duties, 23
    Qualifications, 22
    Salary, 22
Shelf list, 65
    Card, 38, 42, 44-45
    Example, 40-41
Shipments
    Procedures for, 35
    Receipt of, 35
    Return of, 35
"Show and tell", 12
Slides, 70
    Repair, 70
    Symbol, 65
Southern Association of Colleges and Secondary Schools, 4, 73
Space, 1
Space for library facilities
    Audio-visual, 54-57
    Classroom, 54-57
    Conference room, 54-57
    Librarian's office, 54-57
    Periodical storage room, 54-57
    Professional reading room, 54-57
    Reading room, 54-57
    Receiving and sorting room, 54-57
    Restroom, 54-57
    Workroom, 54-57
Specimens, 69
    Symbol, 65
Standards, 50
    Definition, 3
    Elementary school library, 3, 6
**Standards for School Library Programs**, 6
**Standards for School Media Programs**, 6, 21
State Department of Education, 4, 6, 50, 60-61
Story hours, 15
Story telling, 12, 49-50
Student assistant, 23-24
    Duties, 23-24
    Qualifications, 23
    Salary, 23
    Selection, 23
    Volunteer, 23
    Work schedule, 23-24
Student assistant program, 23
    Endorsement by school administrator, 23
    Guidelines for, 23
    Hourly pay program, 24
Students, 46-49, 51
    Average reader, 16
    Browsing, 14
    Gifted, 14, 16
    Slow reader, 13, 15
Subject headings, 36-38
**Subscription Books Bulletin**, 62
Superintendent (state)
    New York, 2
Supplementary materials, 2
Symbols
    Books, 38
    Filing, 44
    Multimedia, 65
Tape retreival systems, 61
Tape transcriptions, storage, 59

# INDEX

Tax for library use, 2
Teacher, cooperation, 12-13, 15, 20, 24
Teachers, 1, 46-51, 61, 75-76
Teachers salaries, 2
Teaching machines, 61
Teaching methods, 2
Technical processes, 29-45
    Definition, 29
Technical services, 46
Temporary charge slip, 71-72
    Example, 72
Tests, standardized, 61
Textbook, 2
Three dimensional, 61-62
Tracings, 38
Transparencies, 70
    Symbol, 65
United States, 1, 4
United States Office of Education, 2, 5
**Using Reference Materials Effectively in Schools,** 19-20
Vertical File, 58, 69
    Circulation, 71
    Symbol, 65
Volunteer assistance, 24
    Program development, 24
    Training program, 24
    Uses, 24
Weeding, 32
West India Company, 1
**Wilson Library Bulletin,** 31
Work slip, 36, 38
Workroom, 53, 56-58
Workshops
    Teachers', 50